Solutions to Your Parking Woes

When the parking lot is overcrowded and there's no place to park, try this chant. It never fails and usually provides a space close to the front door.

**Goddess Mother, lift Your face
And find for me a parking space.**

If you can't remember where you parked the car, close your eyes and chant:

**Ancients, come from near and far,
Find for me my waiting car.**

Open your eyes and look out over the parking lot. Usually, the car comes into view right away.

About the Author

Dorothy Morrison lives the magical life in the boot heel of Missouri with her husband and teenage son. They share their home with two feisty Labrador Retrievers, Sadie Mae and Jonah, various tropical fish, and a large assortment of African violets. She is a Wiccan High Priestess of the Georgian Tradition and founded the Coven of the Crystal Garden in 1986. An avid practitioner of the Ancient Arts for more than twenty years, she teaches the Craft to students throughout the United States and Australia. She is also a member of the Pagan Poet's Society.

An archer and bowhunter, Dorothy regularly competes in outdoor tournaments and holds titles in several states. Her other interests include Tarot work, magical herbalism and stonework, and computer networking with those of like mind.

To Write to the Author

If you would like to contact the author or would like more information about this book, please write to her in care of Llewellyn Worldwide. We cannot guarantee every letter will be answered, but all will be forwarded. Please write to:

Dorothy Morrison
℅ Llewellyn Worldwide
2143 Wooddale Drive
Woodbury, MN 55125-2989

Please enclose a self-addressed, stamped envelope for reply or $1.00 to cover costs. If outside the U.S.A., please enclose an international postal reply coupon.

everyday
MAGIC

SPELLS & RITUALS
FOR MODERN
LIVING

Dorothy Morrison

Llewellyn Publications
Woodbury, Minnesota

Cover design: Cassie Willett
Editing: Barbara Wright
Book design and project management: Amy Rost

FIRST EDITION
Twenty-sixth Printing, 2020

The poems attributed to Merry and Kalioppe are used with permission from these poets.

Library of Congress Cataloging In-Publication Data
Morrison, Dorothy, 1955–
    Everyday magic: spells & rituals for modern living/
Dorothy Morrison. — 1st ed.
        p.   cm.
    Includes bibliographical references and index.
    ISBN: 978-1-56718-469-3
    1. Magic.   2. Ritual.   I. Title.
    RF1623.R6M67   1998
    133.4'4—dc21

Llewellyn Publications
A Division of Llewellyn Worldwide Ltd.
2143 Wooddale Drive
Woodbury, MN 55125-2989
www.llewellyn.com

Llewellyn is a registered trademark of Llewellyn Worldwide Ltd.

Printed in the United States of America

Other Books by Dorothy Morrison

Magical Needlework
(1998, Llewellyn Publications)

In Praise of the Crone
(1999, Llewellyn Publications)

The Whimsical Tarot
(1998–1999, deck and book; U.S. Games Systems, Inc.)

Yule
(2000, Llewellyn Publications)

Bud, Blossom, Leaf
(2001, Llewellyn Publications)

The Craft: A Witch's Book of Shadows
(2001, Llewellyn Publications)

The Craft Companion: A Witch's Journal
(2001, Llewellyn Publications)

Everyday Tarot Magic
(2003, Llewellyn Publications)

Everyday Moon Magic
(2004, Llewellyn Publications)

Everyday Sun Magic
(2005, Llewellyn Publications)

*Dancing the Goddess Incarnate: Living the Magic of
Maiden, Mother & Crone* (with Kristin Madden)
(2006, Llewellyn Publications)

Dedication

To all who instinctively sing to the tune of Nature, dance to the melody of magic, and sway rhythmically to the beat of the Universe.

In Memory of...

My father, Ed, and my sister, JoAnna, whose zest for living was a constant source of inspiration to me. Thank you for encouraging me to follow my heart, for showing me the joys of free-spiritedness, and for teaching me that the cost of individuality is always worth the price. I miss you both. Rest peacefully until next we meet.

George "Pat" Patterson, founder of the Georgian Tradition and Church of Wicca, Bakersfield, who passed into the Summerland before we could meet, but who left his imprint on both my magical and mundane lives. Your work taught me the magic of diversity. Blessed be, Pat!

elementary concoction

A drop of that essential oil—
Breath of life with which we toil
A grain of sand, a world complete
Within the bottle these do meet.

A spark, a flame, the Muses light
Upon the dark face of the night
A sip, to some, the waters clear
And these, so, too, assemble here.

Within the hazes, from the mists
Gloaming's spawn and Dew's kissed
Bright Ev'n Star and rising Sun
Come one, come all and join the fun!

Merry

Contents

Part One
Ancient Arts, Modern Solutions

Part Two
Modern Magic for Busy Folks: A Grimoire

acknowledgments

*t*he birthing of a book isn't much different than the birthing of a human baby. After the ecstasy of conception, you realize that the actual birth process is a culmination of the influences, efforts, and talents of others, and that you are only the vessel from which the baby is delivered. That being the case with this book, many thank yous are in order but most especially to the following for their roles as midwives, nurses, and birthing coaches.

To the Muses, Who insisted that I take note of Their endless ideas and words of advice, even when it meant jolting me awake in the middle of the night.

To Sarasvati, Goddess of writing, eloquence, and words, Whose steadfast efforts created sentences and paragraphs from even the most vague of thought patterns.

To the Lord, Lady, and Ancients, Whose loving guidance and enthusiastic encouragement prompted me to share these non-traditional techniques with the rest of the world.

To "The Greenman"—my husband and my friend—who constantly inspires me with his love of the woods and his treatment of the sacred rites of life, death, and rebirth.

To my adopted parents, A. J. and Sandy, who love me just the way I am—stubborn streak and all.

To Trish, my friend and mentor, who kicks me in the butt when I need it, makes me laugh when I don't think I can, and inspires me with the wisdom of experience.

To Gay, who taught me that survival of the mundane comes only from living a truly magical life and that, with enough practice, even an Earth Goddess can follow a bouncing ball tossed into the air by the horns of Aries.

To Hannah, Vicki, InaRae, Julie, Endora, Linda Lee, Randi, Vivienne, and all the other members of my extended family who sent long-distance hugs and smiles when I needed them most.

To Arwen Nightstar, who graciously allowed the use of her release rite as a base for the "Pet Death/Euthanization Ritual," and whose stone gifts (even when not originally intended for me) always seem to wind up in my pocket.

To Auralii, who generously shared her "Three Sisters Morning Blessing" and allowed me to re-work it for use in this book, and whose knack for positive thinking and spontaneous gift-giving goes unsurpassed.

But most of all, to you, the reader. Only through your efforts does magic gain immortality and the power necessary to build a better world for future generations.

Heartfelt thanks and loving blessings to you all!

introduction

*t*oday's world is a hectic place and living in it is a busy matter. Whether we work inside the home or out, our daily schedules read more like novels than to-do lists. We rush about desperately trying to meet our agendas, manage personal lives, tend to loved ones, and maybe even eke out a little time for ourselves. It is an impossible feat. At the end of the day we succumb to exhaustion, and all we can think about is falling into bed. Who has time to practice magic?

In the days of our forefamilies, the practice of magic didn't seem to present the scheduling dilemma that it does today. Although life took on a slower pace, workloads were just as heavy. For our ancestors, a normal day involved rising early, getting to bed late, and a constant flow of hard, back-breaking work in between. Even worse, they didn't have today's technology to provide workable solutions to everyday problems. As a result, they probably had less spare time than we do today. Still, they found time to practice the Ancient Arts.

How on Earth did they do it?

Our forefamilies saw the practice of magic as a lifestyle rather than an individual set of events. They wove its power into every fiber of their day and it lived within every breath they drew. Hence, the separation between the worlds of the mundane and magical was virtually nonexistent. Every act—cooking, cleaning, plowing, even sleeping—became a magical operation and its completion was a reason for celebrating the Gods.

Living the magical life is a simple matter of taking a fresh look at what magic is and what it isn't. To start with, magic is not a practice.* It is a living, breathing web of energy that, with our permission, can encase our every action. It is not an exhausting process and doesn't make our lives more difficult. Instead, it smoothes our path, increases our energy, and raises our production levels. Most important, though, magic is a time-saver. Incorporating it into our fast-paced, technologically driven lives can cut our workloads and provide us with the extra time we need for fun, rest, and relaxation.

But how can something so ancient mesh with a technology-based world? The answer is simple. Magical energy relies upon the same force that supports much of

---

* Only for lack of a better word do I use the term *practitioner* throughout this text. It is a word commonly used to describe those who work with the Ancient Arts.

technology: electricity. A quick refresher course on the Elements and Their vibratory forces gives us proof.

A magical force that we can see and hear flows through the core of the Fire Element and gives It life. We see it in the lithe, dancing movement of the flame and hear it pop and crackle on the hearth fire. Because it reacts similarly to electricity and holds a positive charge, this force is known as electrical fluid. It relates directly to the expansion qualities of Fire.

Unlike Fire, magnetic qualities flow through the matrix of the Water Element. We feel them in the river current and see them when the tides roll in at the rise of the Moon. This force is called magnetic fluid. It holds a negative charge and is directly linked to the shrinking and contracting qualities of Water.

The Air Element has a special relationship with both Fire and Water. It nourishes and strengthens Fire. It changes the density of Water, transforming It into fog, rain, sleet, and snow. Even though Fire and Water live on opposite poles, They can mix to form steam, smoke, and lightning, but not without the help of a mediatorial bridge or ground. Air provides the grounding force between the two.

The Earth Element contains the Elements of Fire, Water, and Air in Their most solid forms. Together They form rock, lava, and glaciers; They make our soils rich, moist, warm, and dusty. Because Earth actively involves the other three Elements and takes its life source from Their combination, we call its force electromagnetic fluid.

When we work with the forces of the Elements—a basic to natural magic—we put together all the necessary components for static electricity. Whether they know it or not, even the most stringent practitioners of the Old Ways, like their forefamilies, work with technological forces. Because these forces already exist in an underlying fashion, there is nothing to prevent a "surface" combination by involving them directly and allowing them to help us in our efforts toward successful magic.

Looking at magic from this angle sheds a different light on its practices and benefits. Realizing that magic already shares a common element with technology opens a wealth of possibilities for the use of modern convenience items as magical tools. This in itself saves time, money, and effort—all short supply commodities in our busy world. Couple that with the fact that magic has the capability to solve many technological problems that we encounter today, such as computer crashes, machine malfunction, and traffic difficulties. Soon, the matter of whether today's lifestyle provides enough time for magical use flies right out the window. The issue becomes, instead, whether we really have the time *not* to incorporate it into our lives. Personally, I don't think we do.

Ancient Arts

MODERN SOLUTIONS

part one

bottles and jars of this and that

Bottles and jars in the cabinet kept
Sung free one ev'n, they danced and leapt
A joy! To be filled! A wish come true!
Petals and shells and waters so blue
From the world so wide come grains and sands
Sprinkles of words from myriad hands.

Jars and bottles from the cabinet flew
A use, a use, one old but new
The song and the dance went on all day
Children of the cabinet come out to play
Clear, shining, and clean, some without lid
Dusty, cloudy, unwashed, "Come," they bid.

Merry

chapter one

Magical Boosters

*A*lmost anyone can work a spell, and you don't have to be a genius to obtain successful results. All spellwork requires is solid intent, concentrated focus, and the ability to channel energy toward the specific direction of your wishes. Be that as it may, the end results don't always parallel the original vision, and if a spell doesn't come to fruition in twenty-one days or less, chances are it won't work at all. Why? Because certain cosmic forces can affect our magical efforts, and if the conditions aren't right, even the most carefully planned spell can fizzle out before it ever reaches its target.

Working with magical boosters is a good way to prevent such an occurrence and increase the chances of magical success. For example, the day of the week or time of day you begin a spell could provide the proper conditions to set the magic in motion. Using a particular Element or color in the spellwork might speed the results. Even the way the wind blows can make a difference in magical impact.

Atmosphere and the Working Environment

Creating an atmosphere conducive to spellwork is probably the most important step you can take toward successful magic. Atmosphere puts us in the mood, molds the frame of mind, and builds anticipation. Trying to work in an area that doesn't have a magical flavor is a little like trying to build a house without a hammer. Things just don't hold together well.

Building the proper atmosphere for magic isn't difficult, and there is no wrong way to do it. All it takes is a small space, a little imagination, and a few items that say "magic" to you.

Some folks like to use an altar to create a magical environment, because it reminds them that spellcasting is a spiritual kind of work. They erect formal altars and include candles, incense, and symbols of the Lord and Lady. Others go for a more informal look, constructing a space that doesn't look like an altar at all, but more like an arrangement of interesting objects. One of my altars, for example, contains a miniature rocking chair made of grapevine and dried flowers, a basket of dried pomegranates, an antique doily, a cobalt blue perfume bottle, several packets of seeds, and an assortment of crystals and stones. The fact that it doesn't look like an altar in no way hampers its magical value. In fact, some of my most successful work began in that very space.

Constructing an altar isn't the only way to create a magical environment. Some of the most sacred spaces in my home include a bookshelf covered with building-block castles, a large wooden spice cabinet, a shelving unit filled with African violets, and the wall that faces my computer desk.

The point is, the working environment you create doesn't have to broadcast your practices for magical conductivity. The important thing is that you feel its power when you enter the area. Feeling the power makes you feel magical, and the person who feels magical produces potent magic.

Moon Phases

The Moon exudes a cool, feminine, silvery-feeling energy that rules the life-giving waters of our planet—the rains, tides, and dew—as well as those in the physical body, such as menstrual cycles and other bodily fluids. She also rules all emotional responses. Raw, properly focused emotion energizes magic. For this reason, many practitioners work in conjunction with a phase of the Moon's cycle that is in harmony with their magical intent.

◆ Waxing

This phase occurs when the Moon grows from dark to full. In this phase, the Moon provides the proper energy for magical efforts requiring growth or enhancement. It is

a good time for beginnings, fresh starts, and new love and
is of benefit in building businesses, friendships, partnerships, and financial prosperity. The waxing phase also
provides suitable conditions for planting herbs, develop-
ing psychism, and increasing physical health and well-
being.

To seal spells performed during the waxing Moon, use
this chant or one of your own choosing:

> **Oh, Maiden Moon, now hear my plea:**
> **Hearken, hearken unto me!**
> **As you grow, my spell enhance—**
> **And power its magic with Your dance.**

◆ Full

The Moon's energy is most intense when She reaches
abundant fullness. Any magical effort, especially difficult
ones, can benefit greatly from the potency of this phase.
Use the full Moon to amplify magical intent and to give
spellworkings additional power.

To seal spells performed during the full Moon, use this
chant or one of your own choosing:

> **Abundant Mother, Moon so bright**
> **Hear my plea upon this night.**
> **Your fertile power lend this spell;**
> **Make it potent, strong, and well.**

◆ Waning

The shrinkage of the Moon from full to dark is called the waning phase, and it offers an energy suitable for recession, peaceful separation, or elimination. Use the waning Moon to end undesirable eating patterns, break bad habits, or to remove yourself from dysfunctional partnerships or stressful situations. Its energies favor any magical effort requiring decrease or removal.

To seal spells performed during the waning Moon, use this chant or one of your own choosing:

> **Oh Aging One of grace, now hear:**
> **With your guidance, this spell steer.**
> **Remove all blocks and hesitation,**
> **And take it to its destination.**

◆ Dark

Some practitioners use this phase as a period of rest. They find it useful for regeneration, relaxation, and gathering for the creative phase of the waxing Moon.

Others prefer to use it for meditation, psychic power enhancement, or for delving into past life memories to help them better understand current difficulties. Dark Moon energy also lends itself to divination and matters where truth is an issue.

To seal spells performed during the dark Moon, use this chant or one of your own choosing:

> I call on You, Oh Crone so wise—
> One Who rules the darkest skies.
> Come and be my treasured Guest,
> And aid me on this magical quest.

Sun Phases

The Sun emits an uncomplicated, direct masculine energy that is warm and golden-feeling. Unlike the Moon, He moves through several different phases every day, availing the practitioner of unlimited opportunities for immediate spellwork. His wide range of properties can boost almost any magical effort normally aided by the Moon.

◆ Sunrise
Sunrise lends its energies to beginnings, change, and cleansing. This phase is beneficial to magical workings that involve new endeavors in employment, love, or direction in life. Rejuvenation matters such as renewing hope and trust, good health, or even mending a broken heart also benefit from this energy.

To seal spells performed at sunrise, use this chant or one of your own choosing:

> **Oh, Youngest Babe, so newly born,**
> **Help me on this bright new morn.**
> **Aid this spell with Your fresh power,**
> **And strengthen it with every hour.**

◆ Morning

During the morning hours, the energy of the Sun expands and becomes strong and active. Any project that requires building, growth, or expansion works well during this phase. This is an excellent time to build upon the positive aspects in your life, to resolve situations where courage is necessary, and to add warmth and harmony to your home. Morning-Sun energy is also of benefit when performing plant magic or working spells for financial increase.

To seal spells performed in the morning, use this chant or one of your own choosing:

> **Oh Brother Sun of growing strength,**
> **Come to me and stay at length.**
> **Wrap this spell with intensity,**
> **And add to it Your potency.**

◆ Noon

The influence of the Sun reaches its peak at high noon. This vibration is excellent for performing efforts that involve the mental abilities, health, and physical energy. It is also of value when charging crystals, stones, or metal ritual tools such as athames, censors, and cauldrons.

To seal spells performed at midday, use this chant or one of your own choosing:

> **Father Sun, of strength and might,**
> **Aid this spell in taking flight**
> **To its target, now please guide—**
> **Increase its power as it flies.**

◆ Afternoon

As the Sun journeys downward, His energies take on a receptive quality. Use this phase to work efforts involving professionalism, business matters, communications, and clarity. It is also of benefit for spellwork involving exploration and travel.

To seal spells performed in the afternoon, use this chant or one of your own choosing:

> **Aging One of Amber Light:**
> **Hearken! Hear me! Aid my plight!**
> **Take this spell where it must go,**
> **And give it power that it might grow.**

◆ Sunset

The predominant energies of sunset provide a suitable condition for spellwork requiring reduction or alleviation. This phase lends itself to the removal of stress and confusion, hardship, and depression, and the disclosure of deception. It is also a good time for dieting magic.

To seal spells performed at sunset, use this chant or one of your own choosing:

Oh Setting Sun of passing day,
Aid me in Your gentle way.
Take this spell, oh Ancient One;
Give it Your strength as You pass on.

The Winds

Harnessing the power of the winds can add incredible intensity to magic. The vibrational gifts of the winds differ according to the direction from which they blow, allowing the practitioner a vast assortment of energies for spell-work. If you can't tell which way the wind is blowing, simply hang a windsock outside your window.

◆ East Winds

Easterly winds provide an excellent opportunity for spell-workings involving change, transformation, new beginnings, and fresh perspective. They also lend their power to inspirational, communicative, and creative ventures. They provide the perfect conditions for spell-writing, ritual creation, and talking things over with your Spirit Guide.

◆ South Winds

Though most commonly used by magical practitioners for relationship spells involving love, lust, and passion, southerly winds provide us with many other opportunities. They furnish perfect background conditions for efforts involving vitality, initiative, courage of conviction, and determination, as well as those in which anger, jealousy, and selfishness need to be resolved.

◆ West Winds

Winds that blow from the West have a healing, cleansing quality, making them good conductors for spellwork involving issues on both the physical and emotional levels. They also offer conditions conducive to strengthening the intuition and to efforts involving both mental and physical fertility and productivity. Some practitioners also use this wind for working with matters of the heart.

◆ North Winds

The cold strength of northerly winds provides a suitable condition for performing efforts of a practical nature. They provide good conditions for working with financial or home management matters or issues where keeping a level head is important. When these winds blow, it is a good time to plan spells you intend to work when the wind changes.

Days of the Week

Each day of the week is ruled by a different deity and has an energy field and vibration all its own. For this reason, some magical practitioners like to perform spells on a day in harmony with their intent. Working with the vibrations of a specific day is a great way to increase the effectiveness, power, and success of spellwork.

◆ Sunday

The first day of the week is ruled by the Sun. It is an excellent time to work efforts involving business partnerships, work promotions, business ventures, and professional success. Spells where friendships, mental or physical health, or bringing joy back into life are an issue work well on this day, too.

◆ Monday

Monday belongs to the Moon. Monday's energy best aligns itself with efforts that deal with women, home and hearth, the family, the garden, travel, and medicine. It also boosts rituals involving psychic development and prophetic dreaming.

◆ Tuesday

Mars rules Tuesday. The energies of this day best harmonize with efforts of masculine vibration, such as conflict, physical endurance and strength, lust, hunting, sports, and all types of competition. Use them, too, for rituals involving surgical procedures or political ventures.

◆ Wednesday

This day is governed by Mercury. Wednesday's vibration adds power to rituals involving inspiration, communications, writers, poets, the written and spoken word, and all matters of study, learning, and teaching. This day also provides a good time to begin efforts involving self-improvement or understanding.

◆ Thursday

Jupiter presides over Thursday. The vibrations of this day attune well to all matters involving material gain. Use them for working rituals that entail general success, accomplishment, honors and awards, or legal issues. These energies are also helpful in matters of luck, gambling, and prosperity.

◆ Friday

Friday belongs to Venus, and its energies are warm, sensuous, and fulfilling. Efforts that involve any type of pleasure, comfort, and luxury, as well as the arts, music, or aroma (incense and perfume) work well on this day. As Venus lends its sensuous influences to the energies of this day, use it for any magical work that deals with matters of the heart.

◆ Saturday

Saturn lends its energies to the last day of the week. Because Saturn is the planet of karma, this day is an excellent time for spellwork involving reincarnation, karmic lessons, the Mysteries, wisdom, and long-term projects. It is also a good time to begin efforts that deal with the elderly, death, or the eradication of pests and disease.

Color

Color plays a large part in the physical world. It affects the way we feel, the way we act, our decisions, and, often, our energy and productivity levels. A police officer, for example, is more likely to stop a red or yellow car than one of a more subdued color. Women who wear a lot of red and black seem to intimidate people more often than women who wear blues, greens, or pastels. We usually think of men who wear gray suits as being conservative, while those sporting neon colors convey a more liberal message.

Color influences our lives in ways that we don't understand. That is because it pulls directly on our emotions and stirs the tides beneath the surface world. Because of its direct link to the emotional pool, it is no surprise that color also has an intense effect on magical work.

Use the information below as a starting point for incorporating color into magical work. These are only guidelines, so feel free to deviate from them to suit your own tastes and needs.

◆ Black

This color is usually associated with the clergy and ministerial figures. Wearing black deters others from gossiping about you, meddling in your affairs, and interfering with your life. Use it in efforts that deal with separation, wisdom, and keeping things hidden from view, as well as for calling upon the Crone aspect of the Triple Goddess.

◆ Pale Blue

Wear this shade when you feel confused, need to clear your mind, or feel out of control. It also works well for magical workings that involve calmness, peace, tranquillity, healing, and pleasant dreams.

◆ Dark Blue

Don this color when you feel the need to get organized and add some structure to your life. Use it in magical efforts to invoke the Water Element or as a general hue for calling upon feminine deities.

◆ Brown

If you have lots of excess energy and need to ground and center, brown is a good color for you. Try it for spells that involve common sense, bringing stability to life, or diffusing a potentially harmful situation.

◆ Gold

Wear gold to make you feel prosperous and secure. Some magical practitioners like to use a gold candle on the altar to represent the God.

◆ Green

To increase your ambition, better accept challenges, and achieve a feeling of independence, wear green. It works well in magical spells that deal with growth, fertility, and prosperity. Use it to invoke the Earth Element.

◆ Lavender

To relax, even in high-stress situations, wear lavender. Use it in magical workings that involve the intellect, soothe erratic energy, and cause inner beauty to radiate outward.

◆ Mauve

To gain co-operation from those around you, wear mauve. It works well in efforts that deal with the intuition, self-trust, and self-confidence.

◆ Orange

To ease the blahs and increase personal motivation, wear orange. Use it in attraction rituals and efforts that involve achieving positive results on academic tests, business projects, and proposals.

◆ Peach

Peach is a safe, unobtrusive, reassuring color. When you wear it, others view you as a non-threatening force in their lives. Try it for magical efforts that deal with kindness, gentleness, sympathy, empathy, and well-wishing.

◆ Pink

Wearing the color pink stimulates self-love and can help you to become your own best friend. This color works well in spellwork that deals with romantic love, friendship, and harmony.

◆ Purple

To gain the respect of others, wear purple. (It is a terrific color for wearing on job interviews.) Use it for rituals involving spirituality, mental ability, and psychic power, as well as invoking the Akasha Element.

◆ Red

Wear red when you need to take charge of a difficult situation. It is especially helpful to shy people who hold positions of authority. Use this color for efforts involving activity, passion, sexual desire, vitality, strength, and energy. It also works well when invoking the Fire Element or the Mother aspect of the Triple Goddess.

◆ Silver

Wear silver to reduce inner turmoil and attain a peaceful state of mind. Some magical practitioners like to use a silver candle on the altar to represent the Goddess.

◆ Teal

This shade balances the practical side of human nature with the Spiritual Self. Wearing it makes you feel like you can handle whatever life throws your way. Try it for efforts that deal with getting a handle on practical matters, making decisions, and achieving balance, or in matters where gaining trust is an issue.

◆ Turquoise

Turquoise is a must for workaholics. Wearing it can help you to step back and put your workload into perspective. Use it in rituals that involve stress relief, study, knowledge retention, and finding the logic in situations where there seems to be none.

◆ White

Wear white to relieve tension and to better focus on your life goals. Use it for workings that require clarity and spiritual guidance, or use it for invoking the Maiden aspect of the Triple Goddess. If need be, substitute white for any color suggested in spellwork; it is a culmination of all colors in the spectrum.

◆ Yellow

Wear yellow if you feel like your opinions and needs fall on deaf ears or you don't feel like you are getting through to someone. It works well in rituals that involve communication, creative endeavors, success, and joy. Also use it to invoke the Air Element and the God.

Words

Words are some of of the most powerful tools available for magic. Their power comes from our constant usage of them for communication purposes. We depend on them to convey facts and opinions. We use them to express ourselves and to share our deepest feelings and emotions. By using them in a repetitive, positive, affirming way, we know that it is possible to change our lives and the lives of those around us. All we have to do is grab them up and put them to use.

Spell wording doesn't have to be pretentious or fancy. The only real requirement is that the words clearly specify the request. When working a protection spell, for example, you might say something like:

Lord and Lady, protect me
from all harm seen and unseen.

This type of wording is simple, but clear and concise. It powers the spell and gives it direction.

Although the example above is effective and leaves no room for cosmic misunderstanding, the use of rhyming couplets (a poetic form in which the last word in each pair of lines rhymes) is also a common technique for many magical people. The practice of using couplets to rhyme spell incantations probably goes back to ancient times. The most common reference to this practice is found in The Wiccan Rede, which says:

To bind a spell every time
Let the spell be spake in rhyme.

How or when this practice began is anybody's guess. But more than likely, it was born of a need to memorize spells at a time when writing them down was unwise and a danger to personal safety. Memorization ease aside, though, the main reason for its continued use probably stemmed from the power it added to magical efforts. Here are a few reasons you may want to consider using rhyming and couplets in your magic.

1. While direct statements guide spellwork, rhyming couplets provide a richer, smoother flow. It is a little like using powdered paint. Dipping your finger in the powder and dabbing it on paper leaves color, but when you add water, a whole new world comes to life. The paint has substance, flows vibrantly across the page, and covers more area in less time. Rhyme does the same thing for spellwork.

2. Couplets give spells rhythm. This rhythm enhances the flow, helps create the altered state of consciousness necessary to powerful magic, and supplies the practitioner with a focal point. We learned about couplets' focused, trance-invoking state when as children we jumped rope to jingles and ditties. The beat of the ditty kept us on track. Yet it often took us to another dimension where all conscious recollection of foot movement escaped. By using rhyming couplets in spellwork, we can transport ourselves to a place between the worlds—the place where magic begins—and still stay focused on the effort at hand.

3. The use of rhyme acts as a flexible sort of adhesive that bundles the pieces of the spell together and holds them in place. This is important because it ensures safe passage of the spell to its final destination, alleviating all possibility of fragmentation or dilution. Using rhyming words in a spell strengthens the magical package we direct into the Cosmos and increases our chances of success.

In short, rhyme is a magical power tool and using it to turbo-charge your work is easy. Take the case of the protection chant example on the previous page. We could easily re-word it to read:

> **Lord and Lady, protect me**
> **From harm I can and cannot see.**

Like the first version, it is specific and to the point. However, the flow, strength, and rhythm of the rhyme give it a power that the other version lacks. Even better, this version is easily committed to memory, a plus for practitioners who like to work without books under their noses.

Anyone can write couplets. You don't have to be a talented poet, and the chant you write need not be a masterpiece. Start by writing your request, then give a few minutes of thought to changing it to rhyming form. Keep it simple, and don't let the search for words overwhelm you.

Working in couplets might take a little more time, but the results are well worth the effort. After all, the more of yourself you put into a spell, the more powerful it becomes.

Symbols

In spellcasting, we combine the power of our intellect, instinct, and imagination with things such as special words, imagery, and the forces of Nature. Sometimes, we even embrace the energy of specific deities and use their power to add potency to our magic. These energies flow into each other and blend together to change the spiritual thought process and bend the mundane attitude. Directed through a symbol, though, they gain the momentum necessary to create the physical reality we desire.

We find symbols in every aspect of life. They come in many forms, such as pictures, objects, gestures, and words. The power of symbols is rooted in their ability to communicate with the unconscious and subconscious minds and to change the way the conscious mind perceives the world.

For instance, if I asked you to define *beetle*, you would probably tell me about a hard-shelled bug. But if I asked you about The Beatles, you would give a much different definition. That is how symbols work—instantaneously and independently of all conscious thought and will. Because they work on many different levels at once, they are capable of transmitting even the most complex ideas in a form simple enough for the conscious mind to accept and understand.

When we channel energy through symbols, the mind manipulates and transforms them into a list of possibilities that is sent directly to the Higher Self. The Higher Self checks the list and decides upon the degree of transformation necessary to reach the desired goal. It chooses an appropriate course of action and sets the spell in motion. Finally, it communicates that information to the conscious mind. Suddenly, we find ourselves doing what we have to do on a mundane level to bring the spell to fruition.

Symbols not only boost spellwork but also provide effective, automatic magic of their own. Working with them is a real timesaver. If you have never used symbology in your spellwork, give it a try. It is the quickest way I know to restructure your personal Universe and reinvent your personal reality.

the nature friends

Trees and flowers, herbs and stones
Share with us their Earthly home.
They live and breathe. They laugh and play.
Some find new homes and move away.
But others hang around a while,
To watch o'er us and cast a smile
Upon us. Then they lend a hand
In spreading magic through the land
By giving us their precious gifts—
Delighting as the Cosmos lifts
Its gauzy veil and spells fly in,
And magic comes back out again—
Then carried on the wings of birds,
A Witch's simple words are heard—
Her voice twirls softly on the winds:
"Thank you all, my Nature Friends!"

Kalioppe

chapter two

The Gifts of Nature

*E*ffective spellwork relies heavily upon focused intent and energy flow. Plant and stone vibrations, like rhyme and symbols, provide assistance in these areas. First, they help the practitioner focus on the intent of the work. This is important, because nothing causes a spell to fall flat more quickly than a wandering mind. Secondly, they add harmonious energy to the work, giving it the impetus to take flight and soar smoothly. Most important, though, the energies of stones and plants reinforce magical intent and give definition to the work. This tells the Cosmos what we want and, to some degree, how we expect it to happen. Because plants and stones express both symbolic and inherent values, incorporating them in magic makes every effort a powerful operation.

Herbs

Herbs are perhaps the most commonly used plants in magical workings. This is probably because they have an inherent strength that many other plants can't boast. Herbs are common, hardy plants that require little tending to thrive. They survive easily within the basic realm of the Elements. All they need is a spot of Earth, Air, a few drops of rain, and a little sunshine for lush growth. It doesn't matter whether you water or fertilize, talk to them or love them. Herbs go on about their life cycles regardless, re-seeding themselves and taking up residence wherever they please. Unlike other plants, herbs are an independent sort. Harnessing that kind of unregimented energy and using it for spellwork brings great power to every effort.

Charging Herbs

For extra power, you can charge the herbs you decide to use in spellwork and imbue them with the magical properties you desire. If you aren't familiar with this process, try the charging method described below.

1. Put the herb in a bowl or saucer; use only the amount necessary for the current spell. Put your hands over the dish and feel the energy rising from the plant. Touch the herb with your dominant hand, close your eyes, and concentrate on your magical need.

2. Hold some of the herb in your hand and rub it between your fingers. Feel the energy exchange flow between your fingers and the herb, charging the plant with your magical need.

3. As you finger the plant, chant something appropriate to your need. For example, if you were charging
dandelions for a creativity spell, you might chant:

Dandelions, so wild and free
Grant me creativity.

Continue to chant until the power grows and the
herb feels tingly to your touch. Repeat the process
with other herbs as necessary.

There are lots of ways to use herbs in magic. A few
ideas are listed here.

• Herbs make powerful charms. Carry a sprig of one
herb or a mixture of several to reiterate your intent to
the Universe.

• Sprinkle powdered herbs through the house or use
them in sachets. Mixed with unscented talc or cornstarch, herbs make good body powders. (**Note:** If
you have sensitive skin or are prone to allergies, test
these powders on a small area of skin before covering yourself with the mixture.)

• Burning herbs quickly fills the atmosphere with
magical intent. Add herbs to incense or roll anointed
candles in powdered herbs.

• The infusion process removes herbal energies from
dry plant material and changes them to liquid form.
Herbal infusions open several doors of opportunity
to the practitioner. Use them as washes to cleanse
the house, add them to bath water, or drink them as
teas. (**Note:** Before you ingest any herb, check with
a reliable herbal source to make sure it is safe for

human consumption. Some herbs are poisonous.) In oil form, use infusions to anoint the body, candles, and ritual materials.

- To change a situation, toss herb seeds on the winds while concentrating on the necessary alterations. As the seeds sprout, transformation begins.

- Growing herbs in or around your dwelling provides a living, continuous form of communication to the Cosmos. It reminds the Universe that the connected spell is ongoing and infinite.

Many common kitchen herbs make powerful additions to magical work. The list below outlines some magically potent herbs that most people keep on hand.

◆ Bay Leaf
Use this herb in efforts that involve athletics, competition, and victory; the removal of negative energy; and protection from illness. It is also useful for wishing, divination, and love spells.

◆ Chamomile
Chamomile* has a multitude of magical uses. Try using it for luck in gambling; prophetic dreams and sound sleep; protection; love; and hex-breaking.

◆ Cinnamon
This common kitchen herb vibrates on a highly spiritual level, making it nearly indispensable to the practitioner. Use it for efforts involving prosperity, love, lust, success, physical energy, and divination.

---

* See herbal warnings, page 311.

◆ Cloves

This herb works well in efforts involving lust, love, luck, and money. Try it, too, for relieving depression, easing grief, and dispelling melancholy.

◆ Ginger

Use this herb in spellwork where the increase of psychic ability, good health, power, or success is an issue.

◆ Lavender

Though primarily an herb of protection, lavender is also helpful in efforts involving childbirth, love, peaceful sleep, healing, and longevity.

◆ Mugwort

Many magical practitioners call mugwort* "the Witches' herb," because drinking the infusion or smoking the dried leaves brings an altered state conducive to the increase of psychic awareness. The infusion is also used as a magical wash for scrying mirrors, crystal balls, and pendulums.

◆ Nutmeg

Try this common herb in spells dealing with love, money, luck, and health.

◆ Sage

Made famous by the Native Americans for its use in smudge sticks, sage* smoke removes negative energy and its residue from areas, buildings, and people. Try it, too, for spellwork involving good health, fortune, wisdom, long life, and wishes.

---

* See herbal warnings, page 311.

Flowers

Although flower energy is lighter than herbal vibrations, it is just as powerful. Floral vibrations stem from the delicate texture of the petals and has little to do with the strength of the plant itself. In fact, some practitioners argue that the energy of flowers is actually more potent than that of herbs.

Flowers are emotional symbols. We use them to denote special transitional occasions like birthdays, weddings, and funerals. We send them as tokens of well-wishing, love, and appreciation. Flowers evoke a strong emotional response from humans, and human emotion is the matrix from which all magic flows. Thus, using flowers in magic increases its potency and effectiveness.

Charging Flowers

To charge flowers and incorporate their energy into magical work, use the techniques listed for herbs. The methods listed below also work well for flower buds.

- Thoroughly wash several flower buds and remove the stems. Add the buds to a glass of water and leave it overnight under the full Moon. Drink the water to receive the magical properties of the flower. (**Note:** As with herbs, check a reliable source to make sure the flowers you have in mind are not poisonous.)

- Write a spell or incantation on a piece of paper. Place the paper beneath the vase of a flower bud that is in harmony with the desire. When the bud blossoms, the magical work is complete.

- Inscribe a candle with your desire and place it next to a flower bud in a vase. Burn the candle continuously, replacing it if necessary, until the bud opens. The blossoming of the bud sets the spell in motion.

For your convenience, a partial list of flowers that are used often in magic is given here.

◆ Honeysuckle
The fragrance of this flower promotes joy, relieves depression, and works well in efforts to increase psychic awareness, finances, and good luck.

◆ Iris
This flower is sacred to the Goddess of the same name, who tends the bridge between life and death. Therefore, it works well in efforts that deal with reincarnation and contacting departed loved ones. Use it also in spells that involve gaining courage, bringing wisdom, relieving stress, or alleviating depression.

◆ Jasmine
No other flower can top the powers of jasmine to promote self-love and self-confidence. It is also helpful when invoking deities of the feminine gender.

◆ Lily
Use this flower for efforts involving strength, protection, and purification. It is also effective for breaking hexes and for keeping away unwanted guests.

◆ Rose

This flower works well in spells involving love, luck, protection, and beginnings. Its heady fragrance is also conducive to prophetic dreaming and the enhancement of psychic abilities.

◆ Sweetpea

Try this flower when working efforts to promote strong and joyful friendships. Also use it in efforts where getting to the truth is an issue.

Trees

Trees play an integral role in day-to-day living. From a mundane standpoint, they provide shelter from the Elements, give comfort in the form of furniture, and produce the oxygen necessary for normal breathing. Trees are also a mainstay in magical work. Practitioners use their leaves, flowers, roots, and bark for incenses and oils, and use their wood to construct a variety of magical tools. Without them, life—both mundane and magical—as we know it would cease to exist.

Sometimes we are lucky enough to find the gifts of the tree already lying on the ground. More often than not, though, we find ourselves harvesting their products for magical use. The collection process isn't as simple as just taking what we need. Trees are living creatures that eat, drink, breathe, and rest. Like the members of humankind, they communicate and have individual personalities. For these reasons, we owe them the same respect and consideration we give our human siblings.

Harvesting from Trees

The first step toward successful harvest is to form a relationship with the tree. Talk to the tree and tell it something about you. Listen as it talks to you and learn something about it. In short, treat the relationship just as you would any other new friendship—with respect, interest and kindness.

The next step is to ask permission to harvest. This is not as silly as it sounds. Consider how you would feel if someone took your belongings without asking. The same is true of the tree. It deserves the same respect you expect for yourself. Tell the tree exactly what you want and why you need it, then wait for an answer. If the tree resists, don't be alarmed. There might be a good reason for its decision, such as ill health, bug infestation, or simply being unprepared. Form a relationship with another tree, but don't discontinue the friendship with the present one. There is always room for one more friend, and who knows what you might learn from the original relationship.

Once the tree grants permission, it is important to consider your harvesting technique and timing so you don't cause the tree any more discomfort than necessary. A sharp knife works well for obtaining leaf, flower, or bark material. If you need to cut branches or limbs, though, try a saw with freshly sharpened teeth. (Garden shears tend to pinch the branch and hinder future growth.)

If you don't need branches immediately, schedule the harvest during the winter months. (Trees are dormant during this season and achieve a state of "numbness" similar to that which humans experience under general anesthesia.) If time is of the essence, though, try the following procedure. It is safe, harmless, and won't injure your tree-friend.

1. Cast a protective Circle around the tree, encircling all visible portions of the root system. (If you have never cast a Circle before, hold the wand, athame, or saw in your dominant hand and face East. Extend your dominant arm fully and walk deosil [clockwise] around the tree while visualizing a neon blue light springing up from the ground. Say something such as:

   Protect this Life, this Tree, my Friend,
   From hurt, disease, and harmful end.

   To complete the Circle, continue walking until you reach the East again.)

2. Select the branch, then tie a cord or rope around it about a foot closer to the trunk than the place you intend to cut.

3. Tap the end of the branch three times with your wand or athame (the side of your hand or the saw handle works, too) to chase its spirit into the trunk or lower branches. Say:

   Oh, Spirit of this Tree, my Friend—
   To lower portions now descend
   Until I've done what I must do,
   So no harm or damage comes to You.

4. Cut the limb quickly and smoothly. Remove the rope.

5. Hug the tree and call its spirit back, saying:

> **Oh, Spirit of this Tree, my Friend—**
> **I call you home! Come now! Ascend**
> **Into the form you've always been.**
> **Be well and live and grow again!**

6. Thank the tree for its gift and give it a gift in return. (While some folks like to leave cornmeal, tobacco, or new pennies, I like to fertilize when working with trees. If you would like to try this but don't have time to fertilize the tree thoroughly, shove five or six plant food sticks into the ground at the base of the tree. Your gift-giving friend will appreciate that much more than an offering of new copper!)

7. Release the Circle by holding the wand, athame, or saw blade in your dominant hand and facing East. Extend your dominant arm fully and walk widdershins (counterclockwise). As you walk, visualize the blue light fading into the ground again. Say something such as:

> **Blue light fade into the ground,**
> **Sealing now this Circle round.**
> **Make this Circle disappear,**
> **So no one knows the magic here.**

The ritual described above isn't necessary when harvesting leaves, bark, or flowers, but always remember to give the tree a token of your appreciation. Your relationship with the tree, like every friendship, is best nurtured with kindness, love, fairness, and mutual respect.

When using trees in magic, try the methods suggested for herbal use. Every part of the tree works well in magic, but some parts work better than others for particular kinds of efforts. To get maximum effectiveness for spell-work, try the following set of guidelines.

- If it grows below the earth (roots and root bark), use the gift for matters concerning the mundane and the practical, as well as for achieving stability and grounding.

- If it grows on the trunk (bark and moss), try it for efforts of healing the physical, mental, and emotional bodies.

- If it towers into the sky (leaves and flowers), use the gift for magical workings involving freedom, divine guidance or intervention, and the planets.

Like all life on this planet, the vibrational energies of trees vary from species to species. A partial list of trees commonly used in magic is given here.

◆ Apple

Sacred to Aphrodite, the apple tree is magically famous for its properties of attraction, love, and seduction. The powers of the apple tree are so strong that for many years bridal bouquets were constructed mainly of its blossoms. When sliced crosswise, the fruit reveals a perfect pentagram (Figure 1). This symbol links it to our Craft and reminds us of the fertility of the Ancient Arts.

Figure 1.

Use materials from the apple tree when working magical efforts involving love and romance or to add "oomph" to any spellwork.

◆ Birch

The budding of the birch tree, sometimes called "Lady of the Woods," heralds the beginning of the agricultural season in many parts of the world. The Earth Mother takes a personal interest in any request made beneath this tree and delivers speedy, positive results when Her name is mentioned in its connection. The birch is also sacred to Thor. Take care when harvesting its bark or wood, for stripping the tree is said to anger Him. For this reason, many magical practitioners believe that birch products should be collected from a tree struck by lightning or from branches that lie on the ground. Use the gifts of this tree for work connected to new beginnings.

◆ Fir

Because the needles of the fir tree are green year round, its energies vibrate toward immortality and infinity. Use the gifts of this tree for "freshening" life, adding zest and vigor, or obtaining a clean bill of health. These gifts also aid rituals involving karma and reincarnation.

◆ Grapevine

Sacred to Bacchus, the grapevine offers the most joyous vibrations of any of the magical woods listed here. This is because the fruit of the vine is generally used to make wine, the consumption of which alters the state of consciousness to levels of mirthful happiness seldom known on the current plane. Use grapevine in any type of celebration or festivity.

◆ Hawthorn

Once burned to purge the Roman temples of negative energy, this tree is best known for its properties of purification. Its branches make excellent smudge sticks for new houses, sick rooms, and magical working areas. The leaves, thorns, and bark work well in any magical effort devised to break old habits or rid oneself of negative energy. Sacred to the fairies, hawthorn flowers make a powerful amulet when seeking freedom of any kind.

◆ Hazel

For centuries, the branches of this tree have been used as divining rods to locate water and important minerals, giving it a reputation for eternal wisdom. Use the gifts of the hazel in efforts designed for knowledge retention, cutting through deceit, or for a more complete comprehension of the Mysteries.

◆ Oak

Long a symbol of the male principle, the oak tree stands solidly against the harshness of the Elements. The white-berried mistletoe growing amongst its branches represents the semen of the Lord of the Forest. Some folklorists say that catching a falling leaf ensures complete freedom from colds and flu all winter. Use acorns in magical works to protect you and yours from all harm and to attract money. Carrying a gift of this tree on your person brings general good luck.

◆ Rowan (Mountain Ash)

This tree vibrates toward life and protection. In ancient times, people planted it by their cottage doors to ward off evil. When ground into incense or brewed into a body wash or oil, the leaves and berries of the rowan tree can do wonders to increase psychic powers and divination skills. Kept in the house, the twigs protect from lightning and storm damage. Carried in the pocket, gifts of the rowan tree increase good health, vibrancy, and physical energy.

◆ Willow

The words *willow*, *Witch*, and *Wicca* have the same lin-guistic root, and so are linked to the Craft even in the most mundane sense. The willow is known as the tree of death, and many practitioners construct their first wands from its branches. Its use for the tools of newcomers to the Wiccan/Pagan life is appropriate, for the old life must end before the new life can begin. Sacred to Hecate, the wood of this tree works well in magical efforts designed to separate, end a phase or relationship, or to protect new beginnings. For healing rituals, prepare the crushed leaves and bark for use as a tea, oil, or incense.

Stones

Stones are a part of the Earth, our physical foundation.
They bring firmness to our planet and keep us securely
placed upon its surface. They also give our world texture,
beauty, and shelter from the Elements. In short, stones
provide stability to our physical existence.

Many practitioners like to incorporate stones in spellwork because of the powerful energies sones have. Not
only do they have an innate inner force that comes from
ancient existence, but their power over the human psyche
is also tremendous. For example, many magical practitioners believe that stones have the capacity to choose their
owners, instead of the other way around. Even many non-
practitioners believe that wearing a birthstone is good
luck, that diamonds signify the commitment of marriage,
and that an opal given without loving intent can cause
disaster for its owner.

Stones exude their own kind of magic. Like flowers,
their beauty is often entrancing and easily evokes human
emotion. But the main reason we use stones in magic has
little to do with any of this. We use them because they
form our physical foundation. They link the mundane
world to the magical realm, bringing a stabilizing force to
every magical effort they touch.

Charging Stones

As with herbs, many practitioners like to charge stones for
specific purposes before using them in magical efforts. An
easy method is described here.

1. Grasp the stone tightly in your dominant hand and hold it firmly against your Third Eye.

2. Concentrate on your magical need and visualize it coming to fruition.

3. Chant something appropriate to your need. If you are charging an opal for past life work, for example, you might chant something such as:

Opal, stone of many hues
Bring my past lives into view.

Continue to chant until you feel the stone begin to pulse with energy. A steady, rhythmic "heartbeat" signifies the completion of the magical charge.

If you feel drawn to stones and want to incorporate them in your magical work, try some of the following ideas.

- Steep a stone in water overnight, and drink the water to bring its magical properties into your life. (**Note:** Check a good stone reference book before you do this. Some stones contain toxins.)

- If you make your own candles, add appropriate stones while the wax is still soft.

- Powder stones and add them to incense. (Place the stone in a plastic bag, then inside several paper sacks. Powder the stone using a hammer.)

- Empower stones and carry them with you to get the full benefit of their vibrations.

Gathering a supply of stones for magical use doesn't have to be expensive. Small, tumbled pieces work just as well as their more costly, faceted siblings. You don't need a large supply either, for many stones contain the same properties. Some, such as clear quartz crystal and opal, can even be programmed to work with every imaginable effort.

The following list outlines a few stones that I find useful for magical work. For your convenience, stone colors are noted next to each stone listed.

◆ Amethyst

Color: Deep purple to pale lavender. This stone is excellent for relieving anger, stress, and depression. It relieves insomnia, wards off nightmares, and brings prophetic dreams. Its many magical purposes also include love, self-confidence, freedom from addictions, healing, and spiritual guidance.

◆ Apache Tear

Color: Translucent black. Commonly carried for good luck, this stone also works well for efforts of protection and divination.

◆ Calcite, Orange

Color: Yellow-orange. An amplifier, this stone magnifies any magical vibration it comes in contact with.

◆ Citrine

Color: Golden yellow to rusty brown. Use citrine for creativity purposes, artistic endeavors, promoting inspiration and ideas, as well as for relief from nightmares and escape from the feeling of being overwhelmed.

◆ Fluorite

Color: Blue, clear, purple, or green. Commonly known as "The Student's Stone," the vibrations of fluorite enhance study efforts, mental ability, and knowledge retention.

◆ Hematite

Color: Silvery black. Born of iron ore, this stone is an excellent "grounder" for those who have no outlet for their excess energy. Use it to increase personal magnetism, to promote "invisibility," and to enhance magical efforts involving battle, healing, and protection.

◆ Opal

Color: Iridescent white with multi-colored "lights." Though many people consider it to be unlucky, opal actually improves good fortune when given in love. Called "The Stone of Karma," this stone works well for remembering previous incarnations and their lessons. Because opal contains all colors of the spectrum, it may be programmed and used for spellwork of any type.

◆ Quartz, Clear

Clear quartz is the most common stone used in magic. Programmed properly, it can be used alone for any magical purpose or added to other stones to amplify their properties.

◆ Quartz, Rose

Color: Pink. This quartz is most used for efforts of love and romance and is excellent for promoting self-love. It is also said to cure acne if rubbed on the face.

◆ Sodalite

Color: Deep blue with white veins. This stone vibrates to the spiritual plane. Effective as a healing tool for fear, anxiety, and stress, it is also useful in meditation and the contact of Spirit Guides.

◆ Unakite

Color: Peach and green color combination. Use this stone to find the beauty in life and circumstance, especially when things seem gloomiest. It is also an excellent stone to use for uncovering deception.

Personal intuition plays a large role when using stones, plants, and other gifts of Nature in magic. Use the guidelines in this section only as suggestions. If you feel drawn to use a particular item for a purpose not mentioned or contradictory to those listed above, follow your intuition. After all, it is intuitive guidance and creative deviation that makes any magic your own!

the magical dance

The whir of a blender, a bunch of dried herbs,
Hand-written notes to be closely observed
A heady aroma that fills every room
And dancing in time to the clatter of spoons
Is a drip coffee maker, a potpourri pot,
And a gath'ring of words, flowers, stones, and what-not

Together they bring the magic to life
It twirls and it dips and it spins 'round in flight
It dances 'round outlets and electrical plugs
It sweeps through the hallways and under the rugs
Energizing the Ancient Arts—setting them free
And bringing its power to you and to me

Kalioppe

chapter three

Modern Tools for Ancient Arts

*t*hough the mortar and pestle were definitely useful to our forefamilies, most of us today just don't have the time to sit around grinding herbs. Most of us don't have time to wait several weeks for magical herbs to dry or for ritual oils to fix. Even if we did, who wants to?

Today, we use many types of modern kitchen conveniences to ease our lives. The days of slaving over a hot stove are gone. Gone, too, are the incessant "When is dinner going to be ready?" questions and those "I'm starving" whines. We just yank something out of the freezer, pop it into the microwave, and in a matter of minutes—presto!—dinner is served. We make fancy salads in seconds with the help of the food processor. The blender is a multi-faceted kitchen wonder, and I know of no working person alive who can manage without a crockpot.

With the high availability of such wonders, we would never dream of going back to consistently cooking on a wood stove or, even worse, an open fire. To even suggest such a thing would be absurd. What's more, we use these devices to best serve the needs of our most precious commodity—our families.

Why, then, don't we use them to increase our magical efficiency? It is probably because we get so caught up in the "ancient" part of the magical arts, that it never crosses our minds. We continually seek out obscure objects to use as magical tools because we think we are supposed to. The fact is that magical implements don't have to be ancient to be useful. They don't even have to look like the ritual tools of old. The only pre-requisite for magical tools is that they work efficiently for the jobs we designate.

Today's convenience items have the capacity to increase efficiency in the magical household and cut preparation time in half. Using these time-savers will not decrease magical power. Spending less time on a working does not mean putting less of yourself into it. Saving time does not mean cutting corners. Instead, it means increased productivity and more time for magical work. If you are still concerned about using today's technology for use in the magical arts, here is some food for thought. The mortar and pestle was once a modern convenience, too.

When the Earth was young, grinding grain and herbs was a painstakingly slow process. The only way to accomplish such a feat was to rub the substance between two rocks and hope for the best. Much later, someone invented the mortar and pestle, a vast improvement over the earlier method. It allowed portability, grinding ease, and a greater amount of productivity. At the time, folks probably viewed the mortar and pestle as a modern convenience. Did our forefamilies scoff at the new device? Did they refuse to use it because the ancient way was better? Did they think it would hamper their magic? No. Obviously, they acquired it and used it. If they hadn't, we wouldn't think of it today as one of our most valuable ritual tools.

If you decide to use modern appliances for magical purposes, please remember that they then become magical tools. In other words, using the same appliance for mixing love sachets and frozen margaritas isn't a good idea (unless you are counting more on magic than drink ingredients to pack the intended wallop). Use appliances for magical purposes only, and consecrate them as such. If you don't have extras and don't want to give up your kitchen appliances, check at your local second-hand store or thrift shop. You can usually find appliances in good condition there for a very nominal charge.

The Automatic Drip Coffee Maker

The coffee maker is an essential part of my existence for most of the same reasons it is to other folks. I, like a good portion of the population, am not a morning person. The fact is, I don't like anybody until I've had several cups of coffee. Having to wait for it makes me an unbearable grump. Fortunately, my coffee maker does the trick in three minutes flat. Its speed gives me time to get my wits together before my loved ones—all morning folks, including the dogs—leap joyfully from their beds.

While the device always provided me with an indispensable service, using it for something other than brewing coffee never occurred to me until I had to consecrate my athame. My roommate at the time was having guests over for dinner and refused to let me use the stove. It didn't matter that I needed an herbal infusion for a consecration. I begged. I pleaded. He didn't care. He just went on cooking. Then he gave me one of those looks and muttered something about "...on pain of death...."

At the time, I thought he was a real jerk. But his obstinacy, as aggravating as it was, brought with it the richest of blessings. It jolted me into a creative mode. I grabbed a coffee filter, threw it in the filter cup, and tossed in the herbs. I added the water and flipped the switch. Then I chanted the incantation loudly enough to roust the neighbors. The result was a perfectly balanced brew that simply tingled with magical essence.

The coffee maker not only saves time, but brews flawless infusions, decoctions, and washes. Here are a few tips for using it in magical efforts:

- Do not use the same coffee maker to brew both ingestible teas and poisonous liquids. If you plan to use the device for brewing washes that list ingredients unsuitable for human consumption, obtain one solely for that purpose.

- Between magical brewings, clean the pot and filter cup with hot soapy water and bleach.

- When brewing decoctions, place the root or bark material in a coffee filter, then close the filter securely by tying it with a string or a rubber band. After the brew cycle, place the pouch in the brew pot and leave it on the warming plate for approximately thirty minutes.

The incident with my roommate forever changed my magical life. Yes, I discovered that using the coffee maker for magic saves time and aggravation. But more important, I realized the meaning of magic in its truest form and its relationship to technology. Magic equals creativity. Creativity equals life. This means that life—how we live it and what we do with it—is the rawest form of magic. The technological resources created by humankind have a magic all their own, and incorporating them into personal magic brings an increase of power to every spell performed. Denying that source of magic is tantamount to refusing magical assistance and a hindrance to all efforts of enchantment. It all boils down to one thing. If it works, use it to your best advantage and be glad for the help.

The Blender

Many years ago, I started a small herbal incense business. The idea was to make an inexpensive, all-natural product that burned efficiently without the aid of charcoal blocks. At first, everything went smoothly. I mixed a few herbs, struck a match, and—voila!—instant incense. I wondered why anyone had ever used charcoal to start with. It didn't take long to figure it out, though. I got an order for a specialty blend, and the stuff just wouldn't burn on its own. I discovered that some mixtures either require charcoal or a base ingredient for even burning.

I checked into buying bulk incense base. It wasn't even a possibility. Made of imported bamboo, it was too expensive for my needs. To make matters worse, none of my suppliers had any useable suggestions. In desperation, I finally called the local lumberyard. That is when it occurred to me that sawdust might be a solution. Even better, I could get it free of charge.

Thrilled, I brought home a dozen large garbage bags of base and went to work. The smile on my face didn't last long, though. The recipe didn't burn any better than before. The grind was too coarse and the sawdust took too long to catch fire. I tried refining it with the mortar and pestle. It was an effort in futility. I ran it through a flour sifter. That didn't work, either. The inspiration pool depleted, I sat down to think.

Finally, it occurred to me. If a blender could reduce ice to mere slush, surely it could powder sawdust. I found the machine, tossed in a few tablespoons of wood shavings, and flipped the switch. The result? A finer powder than the most expensive incense base money could buy. My burning problems were over.

Today, the blender is one of my most valuable magical tools. I use it for every grinding, powdering, and mixing job my old mortar and pestle used to handle. It not only out-performs the device, but cuts the preparation time tremendously. In my book, anything that saves that much time in today's busy world has a magic all its own.

The following are a few tips for using the blender as a magical tool:

- When working with dry ingredients, only add two to three tablespoons at a time. This keeps the appliance motor from overheating.

- Always clean the blender between magical mixings. Pour in a tablespoon of rubbing alcohol and a cup of water, then let the blender run for a few seconds. Empty the cup and wipe dry it with a paper towel or cloth. Cleaning in this way removes any herbal oils or extracts, herbal odors, or plant vibrations. It is a good way to keep the leftover energies of one mixture from combining with the next.

- When powdering gums such as dragon's blood and gum arabic, add a few drops of rubbing alcohol before you turn the machine on. This keeps the powder from gumming up around the blades. Don't worry about the alcohol. It evaporates and leaves no vibrational energies to interfere with your magical intent.

- As the blender grinds and powders, focus on the swirling mixture and concentrate on your intent.

Using the blender as a magical tool can open the doors to a whole new realm of enchantment. Incense-making is just one idea. Use it for making magical powders, sachets, potpourris, and anything else that strikes your fancy. Its possibilities are as limitless as your imagination.

Slow Cookers and Electric Potpourri Pots

With the incense-making problems solved, my business blossomed and flourished. Custom orders became a specialty, so it was no surprise when one of my customers came to me with a problem. She was disappointed in the quality of the oils offered by her distributor. They felt sticky and gummy, and, once applied, the aromas faded. She wanted to know whether I could whip up a batch of oils to match the incense properties. I told her I would check into it and began to research the process.

What I found was discouraging. Some of the oil-making processes took several weeks. Others took several months. Some suggested using the heat of the Sun, while others insisted upon the use of a cool, dark area. By the time I finished poring over the piles of books, I was vastly confused. There was not only no agreement factor, there wasn't even a common thread.

After a week of experimentation, I did discover that heat released natural plant oils more quickly than cool darkness. The aromas were weak, though, and it looked like it might take a month or two to produce a strong enough scent. I didn't have that sort of time. I needed oils—good ones—and I needed them quickly.

After several unsuccessful stove-top attempts (and working with a bunch of other ideas too silly to mention) I tried the slow cooker. The results were phenomenal. The oil was strong and held its fragrance. It didn't feel gummy or sticky. Best of all, the whole process took less than twenty-four hours.

Making your own oils in the slow cooker is easier than you might imagine. Use one part of herbal mixture to one part of vegetable oil, and stir well. Check the oil every six to eight hours for scent. If the fragrance isn't strong enough, strain the oil and add another helping of herbs. Repeat the process until the oil is to your liking. (A twelve-hour cooking period usually produces an excellent product.) Let cool, strain, bottle, and label.

Because the process takes several hours, you might want to add a chant of intent to charge your oil while it is heating. For example, a chant for a personal love oil might go something like:

Oil of Love, enchanted be.
Bring a perfect love to me.

The chant doesn't have to be long or involved to work well. For maximum effectiveness, chant when first adding the mixture to the pot and again every time you stir or add new herbs.

Try these tips when making magical oils.

- Consecrate your slow cooker or potpourri pot as a magical tool and use it only for magical purposes.

- Use the lowest setting available on your appliance. This keeps the herbs from scorching.

- Use a light, unscented vegetable or fruit oil instead of a glycerin-based product. I like grapeseed oil or jojoba oil for making oils of quantity. They don't turn rancid like some of the heavier vegetable oils. For oils that you intend to use quickly, regular cooking oil is fine.

- When working with fresh herbs, bruise them first to release their oils. The easiest way to bruise herbs is to place them in a plastic bag and pound them a few times with the side of your palm. Then empty the contents into the pot.

- Keep the lid on the pot except when you're checking for aroma. Wipe the moisture from the inside of the lid before you put it back on the pot.

Recipes

The recipes that follow work well for magical powders, sachets, bath salts, potpourris, incenses, and oils. They are **not** designed for human consumption. Let your nose be the judge when deciding upon ingredient proportions. This brings your personality into play and makes the blend your own.

For powders, finely grind the herbs together and add them to unscented talc or cornstarch.

Coarsely grind the ingredients for sachets and both dry and simmering potpourris. You may wish to add some essential oils of the herbs listed in the recipe to keep the scents strong in sachets and dry potpourri mixtures.

To make bath salts, fill a plastic bag or jar with rock or pickling salt. Add oils and/or herbs, and give it a good shake. Toss a handful into running bath water.

Burn incense mixtures in their pure forms on charcoal blocks, or mix with sawdust for a self-burning product. If you wish to add some "pop and sizzle" to your incenses, toss a pinch of saltpeter (potassium nitrate) in the mixture. It is available at pharmacies everywhere and makes each incense burning a magical event.

◆ Air

Try this mixture when your practical nature starts to cloud your imagination or override your emotional responses. It also works well for efforts involving new beginnings, risk-taking, and new projects. Mix it with Love (see page 66) to bring a new relationship into your life.

    violet petals
    lavender
    rosemary

◆ Aphrodisia

This is a great mixture to burn in the bedroom if you are looking for a night of passion and wild sex. Having much stronger vibrations than the Lust formula (page 66), it seems to free the inhibitions and creates the perfect environment for sex magic.

    patchouli
    pine needles
    sandalwood

◆ Autumn Equinox

This recipe is a wonderful formula to use when celebrating the autumn season and for rituals of thanksgiving.

    hibiscus
    myrrh
    rose petals
    sage

◆ Attraction
Use this combination by itself to draw general good fortune to you. Add it to any other formula to increase its power and attract the specific result you desire.

cinnamon
frankincense
myrrh
rose petals
sandalwood

◆ Beltane
An excellent formula for celebrating the return of the Sun, balancing the male and female aspects within yourself, and calling upon the Maiden aspect of the Triple Goddess.

almonds
frankincense
rose petals

◆ Candlemas
Though this is a terrific recipe for Imbolc celebrations, it also works well for blessing candles and hearth fires. Used for house-warming celebrations, it imbues the dwelling with a joyful, welcome feeling.

angelica
basil
bay leaves
myrrh

◆ Cleansing

This formula works for avoiding a possible psychic attack. Use it, too, to remove negative energies from your person, belongings, or dwelling.

bay leaves
cinnamon
lemon peel
myrrh
salt

◆ Creativity

This mixture works well when used in conjunction with efforts involving the arts, inspiration, and artistic expression of any kind.

dry, ground coffee
clove
ginger
hyssop
verbena

◆ Dark Moon

Use this recipe when you feel the need to mentally regroup and re-energize. It is great for mental fatigue. Also use it to call on the Crone aspect of the Triple Goddess.

anise
camphor
lavender
wormwood

◆ Divination

This formula is excellent for divination efforts and for workings that require cutting through deception to get to the truth of the matter.

    patchouli
    wormwood

◆ Earth

Use this combination for magical efforts of a practical nature or for personal grounding. Mix it with Money Draw (page 68) for rituals involving financial security. Anoint pet collars with the oil for added protection of your dogs and cats.

    basil
    chamomile
    cinnamon
    juniper berries
    nutmeg
    patchouli
    rosemary

◆ Fire

The Fire formula works well for efforts that involve an increase of activity. Use it, too, for procrastination problems or a personal boost of physical energy.

    cinnamon
    ginger

◆ Full Moon

Use this mixture to invoke the Mother aspect of the Triple Goddess, and for any working that involves abundance and fertility.

anise
lavender
rosemary

◆ Joy

This is an excellent formula for relieving depression. Use it for efforts where enthusiasm, happiness, or friendship is an issue.

allspice
cloves
nutmeg

◆ Jupiter

Use this recipe for any working where general success is an issue. Add it to other formulas for success in all magical efforts.

anise
hyssop
juniper berries
mint

◆ Kyphi

This is a wonderful combination for banishing negative and destructive entities. It also invites good spirits into the household.

cinnamon
frankincense
lotus
myrrh
pine or cypress needles

◆ Lammas

Use this formula for harvest celebrations and for workings where the birth-death-rebirth cycle is an issue.

frankincense
sunflower petals *or* heliotrope

◆ Love

Try this mixture alone, or add it to Joy for strong friendship, Lust (below) for sexual love, or Romance (page 68) for strengthening emotional involvement.

allspice
cinnamon
rose petals
vanilla

◆ Lust

Use this formula for efforts involving sexual arousal and desire. Try it, too, for reviving intimate relationships.

bay leaves
cinnamon
cloves
ginger
vanilla

◆ Mars

This is a great recipe for rituals that involve strength, bravery, the courage of your convictions, or winning some type of battle. Carrying a sachet of the mixture gives timid people the power to stand up for themselves.

dragon's blood
ginger
nutmeg
black pepper

◆ Mercury

Use this formula for magical efforts involving communications, the oral or written word, and knowledge retention. Add it to other formulas when speedy results are desired.

cinnamon
gum mastic
spikenard
vanilla

◆ Midsummer

Try this combination for calling upon the faeries, sprites, brownies, and elves. It also doubles as a good all-purpose formula for magical work of any sort.

chamomile
lavender
mugwort
rose petals

◆ Moon

A great mixture for harvesting emotional energies. Use it for rituals involving women, their cycles, or the feminine aspect of oneself. Mixed with the Love (page 66) formula, it brings great emotion to relationships.

camphor
wormwood

◆ Money Draw

Some people call this formula "Wealthy Way." Use any form of the mixture in conjunction with prosperity spells, and anoint your paper money with the oil.

bay leaves
cinnamon
frankincense
orange peel

◆ Neptune

This is a wonderful recipe for invoking sea spirits and deities, and for putting rhythm and balance back into your life.

ambergris
red poppy

◆ Pluto

Use this mixture for overcoming difficulties that relate to causes of personal importance.

cinnamon
sage

◆ Romance

This is a great formula to bring the light-hearted laughter and fun of romance. Mix it with Lust (page 66) to deepen intimate involvement.

cinnamon
jasmine petals
patchouli
vanilla

◆ Samhain

Use this recipe to tap into the energies of the spirit world. It also works well when contacting the personal Spirit Guide is an issue.

> bay leaves
> nutmeg
> sage

◆ Saturn

Try this mixture for efforts that involve past life recall, reincarnation issues, and understanding life's lessons.

> myrrh
> patchouli
> sandalwood

◆ Spring Equinox

While this is a terrific formula to welcome spring, it can also be used to add warmth and joyful, abundant vibrations to the home.

> jasmine petals
> orris root
> rose petals
> violet petals

◆ Success

Try this combination for any efforts where success is an issue. Add it to other formulas to enhance their properties as well.

> allspice
> cinnamon
> frankincense
> myrrh
> patchouli

◆ Sun

This formula works well for rituals that involve new beginnings, healing and wellness, general happiness, and growth. Use it, too, for calling upon the God or for tapping into the male aspect of oneself.

frankincense
lemon peel
myrrh

◆ Tranquillity and Protection

Wear this recipe to promote a feeling of peace and security. Burn it in the home for its protecting and shielding properties.

basil
frankincense
lavender
lemon balm
rue
thyme

◆ "Take Back My Life"

This is a wonderful combination for rituals that involve taking control of a situation, taking your life back, or opening others up to your ideas or way of thinking.

chili powder
cinnamon
ginger

◆ Venus

Use this mixture to gain assistance from the deities of love and romance.

amber
lavender
rose petals
violet petals

◆ Wishing

This is powerful formula to use in wish magic of any kind.

bay leaves
cinnamon
ginger

◆ Water

This is a terrific mixture for combating indifference and apathy. Also use it whenever you have difficulties bringing your emotions to the surface.

lotus
tonka bean

◆ Yule

Use this formula in celebration of the birth of the Sun or for any working where light overcoming dark is an issue.

chamomile
ginger
pine needles or bark
sage

the spell-caster

Ribbon-tied bundles of herbs hang on hooks,
Bottles and jars, an assortment of books,
Candles and parchment, feathers and stones,
Incense carries a message—through the Cosmos it roams
Toward the home of the Ancients—unnoticed by all
Except those who pay heed to the Ancient Arts' call

Enchantment-wrapped parcels of spells are unleashed—
Gnarled, ancient fingers toward them now reach—
Faded eyes read intentions, consider, and stir
The old Cosmic Cauldron, and magic occurs;
And back on the Earth, power peaks, then it flows
As the spell-caster shouts, "As I will, be it so!"

                                                    Kalioppe

chapter four

Living the Charmed Life

Magical Success

*t*hrough the years, I have seen a lot of magical efforts fall short of expectations, even though all conditions were conducive to success. Why? Because the practitioners involved forgot the basics. There is more to magical success than following a set of instructions, more to it than checking the cosmic conditions, and a lot more to it than using the magical boosters described in chapter one. What the practitioners didn't realize was that all the props in the world won't create magic without concentration, focus, and pure, unbridled desire. When combined, they bring phenomenal results.

One night, I was fortunate enough to witness simple but perfect magic in a local department store. I strolled past the toy section just in time to overhear a three-year-old bargain with her mother for a new toy. Mom was having none of it, but that didn't stop the child. She kept right on, determined to reach her goal and attain success. Just when it looked as if she might lose the argument, the little girl looked into her mother's eyes, firmly set her jaw, and exclaimed, "But Mama! I want it bad for me!" I chuckled, knowing that the toy would find its way into Mom's shopping cart. After all, a magical effort had just reached completion.

If more practitioners of the magical arts would take some tips from that little girl, their success rates would rocket. Unwittingly, the child managed to combine all the ingredients of successful spellcasting and put its magic into effect. She knew exactly what she wanted and focused her energy completely on the goal; moreover, her desire for the final outcome was the strongest I had ever encountered.

When beginning work on any magical effort, remember the last eight words of that tiny child's spell. It is not enough to want to change the world or the path of the Cosmos. It is not enough to know specifically what you want. No, it isn't even enough to focus some energy toward the goal. In order for your efforts to work and work well, you have to want it so badly that you are one with the effort. Once you have become totally attuned to your desire and release that energy into the Cosmos, there is no doubt you will achieve the magical result you crave—the phenomenal results you thought possible only in your mind's eye.

Magic: It's Serious Business

Today's world is full of accomplished magical practitioners, and opinions about the Ancient Arts vary from person to person. No matter the differences, though, they all cling to one common thread: magic is serious business. It is not to be trifled with, played at, or taken lightly.

There are several reasons for this attitude, but most of them have to do with the factors that govern magic and its inner workings. Taking a few moments to consider the following could make a great difference in the way you live the magical life.

Karmic Law

All magic is governed by the laws of karma. This doesn't mean that spellwork can't be enjoyable or fun, only that casting a spell on someone else is tantamount to casting a spell on yourself. Karmic law doesn't work on the equal balance system; instead, it returns to you three times whatever you send out. Because most of us can't stand a triple dose of aggravation, I urge you to consider all options carefully before working magic to control or annoy someone else. With enough planning you can probably find a way to reach your goals without running the manipulative magic gambit.

Ripple Theory

The magical cause and effect system is unlike any other. It works on the ripple theory. A good way to illustrate this is to throw a stone into a pond. After the stone hits its mark, the water settles. In its settling, a related yet independent movement stirs beneath the surface. Ripples appear, radiating outward and encircling water areas previously unaffected by the original stone toss. Such is the case with magic.

This means that every spell a practitioner casts has the capacity to affect hundreds of lives, even the lives of people unrelated to the magical goal. If the spell is beneficial to all, there is no problem. But what if it isn't? And how can we possibly know what is good for people we haven't even met?

Keeping this in mind, even a spell for world peace could have its drawbacks. For example, the closing of steel factories, rubber plants, and clothing mills (formerly busy catering to military needs) would lead to the loss of millions of jobs. The streets would overflow with the previously employed, now homeless, hungry, and forgotten. It isn't a pretty picture, and the Great Depression of the 1930s grows pale in comparison.

Does this mean that all magic is bad and that we shouldn't practice at all? No. It does mean that we need to be absolutely certain of what we want before beginning any magical work and very specific in our requests of the Cosmos when we set a spell into motion. Even so, how can we guarantee that our magic won't harm someone?

One idea is to bind every spell with a safeguard against harm. This not only protects others from magical fall-out, but also keeps the energy flow of the spell directed toward your goal. If you aren't familiar with bindings, try the one that follows. It is direct, to the point, and the best insurance I have found against harming others.

> **By karmic power of number three,**
> **This spell tied and knotted be;**
> **So that its contents stay together,**
> **And can't harm human, beast, or weather.**

Personal Power

As magical practitioners, we seldom realize the full extent of our personal power. In certain instances, magic can reach fruition without the use of props such as candles, herbs, stones, or incantations. It is rare, but it does happen, and a strong emotion (like anger) is usually the driving force that brings the magic into being. I call this "unconscious magic," because in cases like these the practitioner doesn't have the slightest idea that a spell is in progress.

For example, every time one of my friends gets mad enough to cry, we experience heavy rains and thunderstorms. It is lucky for those of us who live here that her crying spells don't happen often or last long and that the resulting storms have never caused harm, damage, or population evacuation.

But if you think a little rain isn't so bad, consider this. Another friend of mine took her dog to a trainer. The dog was lovable and intelligent, but stubborn. The trainer was not used to dealing with stubborn animals, and the two took an immediate dislike to each other. The trainer insisted that the dog was not trainable, and the pet came home early, untrained and skittish.

Days later, the woman took the dog to another trainer, only to discover that her pet, previously an excellent retriever, was absolutely terrified of the retrieval dummy. It didn't take a genius to figure out that in his frustration, the original trainer had beaten the dog with one.

To say that my friend was angry is the supreme understatement. She was livid. Incensed. Positively out of control. Wanting to make sure that the man never abused another living creature, she explored all options. Knowing that magic wasn't feasible, she looked toward the mundane for answers. But nothing she could think of—at least, nothing legal—seemed harsh enough. Finally realizing that she was in no frame of mind to take any sort of reasonable action, she went to bed and resolved to make a decision in the morning.

The next day dawned bright and sunny. My friend was much calmer. She decided to have the trainer's program and facility investigated, and set about collecting phone numbers for the proper authorities. Just as she reached for the phone to make the first call, it rang. The trainer had been hit by a truck. Though the accident wasn't fatal, the man's injuries were serious enough to keep him from training dogs for a while.

Coincidence? It is doubtful. The laws of physics tell us there is no such thing. "Coincidence" is something we use to excuse life events that we don't understand and don't want to deal with. The more likely story is that my friend's conscious mind was so inundated with desperation and emotion that they bled over to her unconscious mind. Her unconscious mind simply took up the cause and remedied the situation for her.

To keep this sort of thing from happening we have to learn to control our emotions instead of allowing them to control us. This isn't always easy. If you have trouble putting emotional response in check, involve yourself in something, anything, and temporarily remove yourself from the situation. Once in a calmer frame of mind, go back to the dilemma and set about solving its problems. After all, effective resolution and level-headedness walk together. Just remember that you are the magician, and, as such, nothing is beyond your control, not even emotional chaos.

Modern Magic for Busy Folks

A GRIMOIRE

part two

*t*he personal grimoire, or Book of Shadows, is the main-stay of every magical practitioner's existence, for it contains a collection of tried-and-true spells, rituals, and chants designed to ease life. Its indispensability factor doesn't stop there, though. The grimoire also contains other important information, such as home remedies, herbal first aid, and planting advice.

The information in this part of the book reflects a partial collection of the data contained in my personal grimoire, and it is with great pleasure that I share it with you. Tested for workability and effective results, each piece reflects good, reliable magic. Used with confidence, each brings positive results.

Even so, don't be afraid to alter these items to suit your needs, personality, or supply of on-hand materials. Be creative and have some fun. Change the wording, make substitutions (for alternative ingredient lists, see the appendices in the back of the book), or just use them as guidelines to construct your own spells. Above all, follow your instincts and trust your intuition. Instinct and intuition feeds your personal magic and gives it the fertile ground necessary to blossom and flourish.

Abuse

Abuse is a serious matter. When dealing with these sorts of situations, please don't forget that the best solution is often a mundane one. Pick up the phone and call the police.

◆ To Combat Abuse (Mental or Physical)

purple candle	basil
vegetable oil	3 inches red ribbon or yarn
rue	3 inches white ribbon or yarn
clove	3 inches black ribbon or yarn
cinnamon	cloth pouch
bay leaf	

Inscribe the candle with the petitioner's name and birth date, then anoint it with vegetable oil. Roll the candle in a mixture of powdered rue, clove, cinnamon, bay leaf, and basil, while chanting:

Herbs mix and mingle well,
Add your power to this spell.

Put the candle in a holder and place it on the altar.

Gather the ribbons together and tie a knot at one end. Braid them together while chanting:

Maiden, Mother, Crone—All Three
From all abuse (name of petitioner) now free.

Tie a knot in the loose ends so the braid doesn't unravel, then tie both ends together to form a ring. Place it around the candle to form a circle. Sprinkle the remaining herbs around the braid, and visualize the circle growing stronger and stronger until it forms an impassable wall of protection. Then light the candle and say:

From hurts and bruises (name of petitioner) is free
As I will, so mote it be,

After the candle burns all the way down, gather the braid, herbs, and candle drippings, if any, into a cloth pouch. Give them to the petitioner to keep on her or his person as a protective measure.

◆ Charm Against Abuse

Rub an arrowhead with lavender, and carry it on your person to protect yourself from abusive situations.

Acceptance ─────────────────────

(For related spells, see "Change.")

◆ Morning Ritual for Learning Acceptance and Tolerance

This ritual works well for granting you acceptance of matters that you cannot change, and for increasing your tolerance of others' beliefs and opinions. It is also effective against racist attitudes.

Upon rising each morning, light a white candle. Sit down in a comfortable position facing the candle and focus on the flame. Say:

> Gracious Lady, hear my plea,
> Grant me tolerance that I might see
> The need for diversity on the Earth
> And see its value and its worth.
> Help me to find the harmony
> In accepting what is meant to be,
> And replace my negative attitude
> With perfect love and fortitude.
> Gracious Lady, hear my plea,
> As I will, so mote it be!

Watch the candle flame for ten minutes while concentrating on your desire to become more accepting, then snuff the flame.

Perform this ritual every morning for seven consecutive days.

◆ Acceptance/Tolerance/Anti-Racism Charm

6-inch square peach fabric	1 teaspoon rosemary
lepidolite or amethyst	lavender ribbon or yarn
hematite	yellow ribbon or yarn
quartz crystal	green ribbon or yarn
small piece of apple peel	

Place the stones in the center of the fabric. Say:

> **Stones made of Rain, Wind, Fire, and Earth**
> **Bring all the power within your girth.**
> **Bring successful change to me.**
> **As I will, so mote it be.**

Add the apple peel and rosemary to the fabric. Say:

> **Fertile gifts of Earthly fruit**
> **My attitude, I ask, transmute**
> **Into a more accepting one**
> **As I will, the spell's begun.**

Gather the edges of the cloth together and tie the pouch closed with the ribbons.

If the charm is for learning acceptance and tolerance, hold it to your forehead and say:

> **To accept and tolerate is the key**
> **To being whole and setting free**
> **The person I was meant to be.**
> **Instill these qualities within me.**
> **As I will, so mote it be!**

If the charm is for changing your racist attitude, hold it to your heart and say:

> **To live and let live, I must learn.**
> **Help me to respect others as I turn**
> **Gently round on the Wheel of Life.**
> **Replace with love, what once was strife.**
> **Teach me to live in harmony**
> **With all my siblings. So mote it be!**

Carry the bag with you or on your person. When your attitudes improve, bury the bag in the Earth.

◆ **Charm for Acceptance of Change**
To see the beauty in change and to be more accepting of progress, wear or carry a unakite.

Addiction

Most of us don't have the will power to overcome addictions on our own; if we did, addiction wouldn't present the dilemma that it does today. No matter the nature of your problem, please get professional help. Then use the following ritual to help rid yourself of any urges to continue unhealthy behavior patterns.

◆ Ritual to Overcome Addiction

paper and pencil	chrysoprase
wide-tipped black marker	orange calcite or quartz
green candle	fireproof dish or small cauldron
matches or lighter	cloth bag (optional)
hematite	

Write your addiction on a piece of paper, then mark through it with a heavy black line. Put it aside.

Inscribe the candle with your name. Light the candle and say:

> **Healing Ancients, I ask of Thee**
> **Take this pain away from me.**
> **Remove any trace of this addiction,**
> **And heal me of all related afflictions.**

Hold the hematite to your forehead and say:

> **Grant courage now and healing power**
> **Strengthen my will hour by hour.**

Place this stone on the right side of the candle. Lift the chrysoprase to your forehead and say:

> **Stone of joy and happiness**
> **Put my urges now to rest.**

Place this stone on the left side of the candle.

Hold the orange calcite or quartz to your forehead and say:

Amplifier of energies
Magnify their powers, please.

Place this stone in front of the candle.
Stand in front of the altar and turn your hands palms up. Say:

Powers of the Earth unite
Bind the powers of this addiction tight
So it will have no hold on me
As I will, so mote it be!

Take the paper in your hands and say:

Chains that bind me, now break free
I am power, strength, and resiliency
I have the courage to overcome
This addiction—go now—run!
Begone from me! Do not return!
Your power over me, I burn!

Light the paper with a match or lighter, then burn it in the fireproof dish, saying:

By flame of Fire, I'm purified
Of your delusionary lies.
I'm free of you and all the strife
That you once cast upon my life.
I am healed now. I am free.
As I will, so mote it be!

When the candle has completely burned out, carry the stones with you either loose or in a cloth pouch. Repeat the ritual as often as necessary to get control of the problem.

◆ Charm to Ease Cravings

Carrying a piece of staurolite in your pocket eases minor cravings.

Anger

◆ Anger Calming Bath

12 ounces beer	almond oil
pale blue candle	Tranquillity and Protection incense (see recipe section of chapter three)

As the bathtub fills with warm water, pour in the beer. Anoint the candle with almond oil; light the candle and the incense. Before stepping into the tub, inhale deeply. Exhale. Concentrating on the color of the candle, say:

Anger, I command you: Go!
Calming power, through me, flow

Lie down in the tub and completely immerse yourself in the water five times. With each immersion, concentrate on the water washing the anger away. This is also a great chakra-clearing bath.

◆ Anger Relief Tea

This tea works equally well for soothing anger and
the antsiness associated with pre-menstrual syn-
drome (PMS). The mixture lasts indefinitely when
stored in a jar with a screw-on lid.

2 tablespoons catnip*	2 tablespoons lemon balm
5 tablespoons chamomile	4 tablespoons lavender
3 tablespoons rose petals	1½ tablespoons vervain

Mix the ingredients thoroughly. Use two tablespoons
of tea for every cup of water. As the tea steeps, chant:

Fiery anger, go away.
Calmness come, and with me stay.
Soothe my mind so I can think,
Steep peace of mind within this drink.

Sweeten your tea with honey if desired.

◆ To Free Yourself of Anger

Add three tablespoons of mint leaves to one cup of
boiling water. Let the tea steep for six minutes and
inhale the steam as the tea strengthens. Strain, sweeten
with honey, and chant the following over the tea:

Cool my anger, herb of mint.
Honey, sweeten my intent.
My attitude, I ask you, change.
Toss heat of temper out of range.

Drink the tea and feel your anger evaporate.

---

* See herbal warnings, page 311.

◆ To Dissolve Someone's Anger Toward You

When someone is angry with you, visualize a pink heart on his or her chest. Divide the heart into four equal sections, then mentally remove the lower right-hand quadrant. Hold the image for a few moments. This will clear away the anger and make way for reasonable discussion.

◆ Protection from Anger

To protect yourself against the destructive forces of another person's anger, sprinkle powdered passion-flower across your threshold.

—————————————————————— **Anxiety**

(For related spells, see "Depression" and "Stress.")

◆ Anti-Anxiety Tea

Add two teaspoons of valerian root to one cup of boiling water. As it steeps, chant:

> Nervous anxiety, you are dead.
> Roots and water, soothe my head.
> Bring to me your calming peace.
> As I will, so mote it be!

Though very effective, this tea has a strong flavor that some people find unpleasant. To cut the taste, you might want to heavily sweeten it with honey.

◆ Vanilla Candle Spell

Hold a vanilla-scented candle in both hands until the wax feels warm to the touch, then chant three times:

> **Vanilla, chase this mess away.**
> **Keep it far from me today.**

Light the candle; let it burn until anxiety dissipates.

Apathy ────────────────────

(For related spells, see "Empathy.")

◆ Spell Against Apathy

> red candle   powdered ginger
> vegetable oil

Anoint the candle with vegetable oil and roll it in powdered ginger. Light the candle and meditate on the movement of its flame. Watch as it dances, flickers, and revels in activity. Visualize yourself as a flame. Watch as you grow bright, move, reach, and twirl in the air. There is nothing indifferent or apathetic about you. You are fire. You are energy in its rawest power. With the image fixed firmly in your mind, chant:

> **Dancing Flame, rawest Power,**
> **Free me of indifference, sour.**
> **Bring compassion to my soul**
> **And grant conviction of my goals.**

Instill interest, fervor, and devotion,
Confidence and true emotion.
And as I trod life's path each day
Let me help others on their way.

Let the candle burn completely.

◆ Apathy Relief Tea

Use two tablespoons of dried peppermint leaves to one cup of boiling water. As the tea steeps, chant:

Add excitement, herb of spice,
Restore my interest in this life.
Indifference, please, now chase away,
Remove this villain now, I say.

Drink the tea hot. Sweeten with honey if you like.

Attention

◆ To Attract the Attention of Others

At one time or another, we all experience feelings of insignificance. To combat those feelings and to become more visible to those around you, carry or wear a piece of hematite. Having the capacity to draw the attention of others to the wearer, its energies inccrease personal magnatism and give the wearer a new feeling of importance.

◆ To Receive Admiration

To bring admiration and praise, carry a bit of thyme on your person.

Automobiles———————————

◆ To Protect Against Automobile Trouble

Using your finger, mark a pentagram over each tire. Then get into the automobile and visualize a blue pentagram hovering slightly above it, with the top point of the star in the center of the hood. Mentally "stretch" the pentagram until the points flow under the car to encase it and join together in the chassis center.

◆ Automobile Protection Charm

1 teaspoon comfrey	4-inch square white cloth
1 teaspoon cinnamon	red ribbon or yarn
1 pinch powdered garlic	green ribbon or yarn
hematite	purple ribbon or yarn
aquamarine	

Mix together a teaspoon each of powdered comfrey and powdered cinnamon. Add the pinch of powdered garlic, then add the stones to the mixture. As you mix, chant:

Good luck to travel you shall be.
Keep my auto problem free.

Pour the mixture onto the cloth square and use the ribbons to tie it into a bag. Hang the charm from the rearview mirror. As you hang it, chant:

No sickness, troubles, or repairs—
This charm protects you from these cares.

◆ To Keep from Running Out of Gas

This is a great help when you are not sure you can make it to the next service station.

Look at the gas gauge and visualize the needle rising from the empty mark. Firmly chant:

Gods of fuel, expand my gas.
Aid me now—come quick and fast.

◆ Charm for Increased Mileage

To increase gas mileage, empower a quartz crystal with the following chant and carry it in your vehicle.

Stone of perfect energy
To mileage bring efficiency.
Let my carbs work like a top—
No backfire, sputter, snap, or pop.

◆ Charm for Protection from Car Trouble

Carrying a cat whisker in your glove box helps protect against car trouble, theft, accidents, and traffic tickets.

Balance ────────────────────

◆ Prayer to the Elements

Use this prayer whenever you feel out of sorts, have the blahs, or need to find balance in your personal circumstances.

Come to me Air, so fresh and so clean,

Grant mental power—keep my thoughts
sharp and keen.

Bring creativity—bring clarity, too.

Lend your positive aspects to all that I do.

Come to me Water, so flowing and free,

Lend compassion and love and gentility.

Grant understanding and tempers,
please soothe—

And life's little problems, please help
me to smooth.

Come to me Fire, so warm and so bright.

As I walk through this life, my pathway,
please light.

Please help me to live and to love
with pure zest—

Standing up for the Truth,
when I'm put to the test.

Come to me Earth, so rich and so moist,

Bestow, please, Your gifts of serene peace and joy

Grant Your stability and ethical ways,

So I may help others, the rest of my days.

Akasha, please come, and work with these four
And balance Their aspects within me once more.
Transform my life, for You hold the key
To changing me into that which I should be.
Elements of all that live and shall be,
Please spin your spell in pure harmony—
Weaving the threads of my life with ease,
And stitching its fabric with Blessed Be's.

◆ For Emotional Balance

Carry both a red tiger-eye and a hematite with you at all times. The tiger-eye gathers scattered energy, and the hematite grounds and transforms it into a positive, useable force.

◆ Affirmative Chant to Balance the Physical and Spiritual

As within, so without
My harmony exists throughout.
I am one with both these worlds
Within the two, my spirit twirls.

◆ To Maintain Balance

Carrying or wearing a double-terminated crystal or a herkimer diamond helps to maintain perfect balance between the physical and the spiritual realms.

◆ Chakra-balancing Bath

Add a quart of beer to a full tub of warm water. Lie down in the tub and relax. Chant:

> **Yeast and hops, balance and clear**
> **Chakra blockages front and rear.**
> **Wash them away from head to toe**
> **As I will, now make it so!**

Stay in the bath as long as you like, immersing yourself in the water twice. Let the water dry naturally on your body.

Beauty

◆ Beautiful Face Spell

> rose quartz   6 rose petals
>
> bottle of witch hazel

Contemplate your face and its flaws. Visualize your face changing into the face you want. Rub the stone lightly over the problem areas and chant:

> **Stone of beauty, stone of love**
> **Erase imperfection as I rub.**
> **Bring to me the face I see**
> **As I will, so mote it be!**

Open the bottle of witch hazel and insert the stone. Take the rose petals in your dominant hand and say:

> **Venus, One of Beauty rare,**
> **I offer You these petals fair.**
> **Bless them with Your loveliness**
> **And bring the beauty I request.**

Rub the petals over any lines, wrinkles, or facial imperfections, then drop them in the witch hazel.

Cap the bottle tightly and give it six shakes each day for a week. At the end of the week, use it every day as a toner after face washing. As you apply it, say:

> **Imperfections, go away.**
> **Beauty of Venus, come forth today.**

◆ Opal Beauty Spell

Empower an opal with the following chant:

> **Inner splendor, shine right through,**
> **Radiate my beauty, true.**

Rub the stone over your body each day for six consecutive days, then carry the stone with you.

◆ To Affect Hair Growth

To speed hair growth, trim the ends at the new Moon; to retard growth, cut hair during the waning Moon.

Business Success ——————————

◆ Basil Spell

flower pot   basil seeds

soil   water

9 pennies

Fill the pot half full of soil. Using a clockwise motion, form a circle with the pennies, placing them one at a time on top of the soil. As you place each penny, say:

**Money grow and join in force,
Bring new riches from this source.**

Cover the pennies with soil until the pot is full. Plant nine basil seeds, chanting with each one:

**Basil seed, as you grow and sprout
My business shall prosper within and without.**

Water the seeds well, and place the pot in the room where most cash transactions occur. Wrap your hands around the pot and say:

**Copper, earth, and seeds, I now enchant,
I transform you into a money plant.
Grow lush, bring cash, bring success to me.
As I will so mote it be!**

As the plant grows, so will your business.

◆ Spell for Co-operation within a Business

orange candle   Success oil (see recipe section in chapter three)

lapis lazuli

Use the stone to carve the likeness of a spider web into the candle. Still carving, superimpose a pentagram on top of the spider web. If a particular project is the subject of this spell, carve the project name into the candle as well. Anoint the candle with Success oil and light it. Chant:

Cooperation, come to me.
Dissension, leave now. Quickly flee.
Everybody work as one
Until all work's completely done.

Place the stone on the altar and let the candle burn down completely. Take the stone to work with you and put it in a safe place.

◆ Sandalwood Business Proposal Spell

Before beginning work on a business proposal, invoke Sarasvati by chanting:

Sarasvati, Eloquent One
Tend this project 'til it's done
Tend its wording—every phrase.
Make it perfect—every phase.
Make it clear as it can be,
Sarasvati, heed my plea!

Work up the proposal and place it on the altar on Wednesday morning. Light some sandalwood incense, and pass the document through the smoke, saying:

Sarasvati, hear my plea,
Bless this work I offer Thee.

Using your saliva, mark a pentagram on the back of every page. Turn the proposal face up and leave it on the altar.

On Thursday morning, place the proposal in an envelope and prepare it for mailing. Mark a pentagram on the back of the envelope with your saliva and say:

Jupiter, come do Your best,
Claim for this proposal true success.

Put the proposal in the mail.

◆ Charm Against Faulty Decisions

To avoid making faulty business decisions, keep a piece of squill root in your office or the desk drawer of your work place.

◆ Business Attraction Wash

glass jar with screw-on lid   1 pint water
½ cup basil

Place the basil in the jar, add the water, and cap tightly. Put the mixture in a sunny window for three days. On the fourth day, sprinkle the water across the front door, cash register area, and through the merchandise aisles. This not only attracts customers, but also keeps vandals and thieves at bay.

Change

(For related spells, see "Acceptance.")

◆ Spell for Change and Transformational Growth

This is a great spell to perform when you feel like your life is going nowhere.

Carefully pick a dandelion that is in the "fluff" stage. Meditate for a few moments on the growth process of the flower. Think about the changes it undergoes from the time it first pokes its head through the ground, to the stage when it re-seeds itself.

Look at the dandelion and say:

> Oh, dandelion of growth and change
> Transformed from sprout to flower range
> And then to fluff, and then, to seed
> Changing ever, little weed
> Bring positive changes to my life
> Bring them quickly without strife
> Help me grow, too, spiritually
> As I will, so mote it be!

Make a silent wish that your life be transformed into a more positive existence, then blow the fluff from the dandelion. Say:

> **As these little seeds take hold**
> **And sprout from rain and rays of gold,**
> **So my life shall change and sprout**
> **Transforming me within and out.**

◆ Spell to be More Adaptable to Change

If you have difficulty adapting to change and need to learn flexibility, obtain a small block of art clay (the kind that can be baked) in a color that you like. Work it with your fingers. The clay has little pliability at first, so some elbow grease may be in order. As you work the clay, concentrate on learning to accept change. Chant:

> **Just as I change the form of clay**
> **My attitudes can change today.**
> **Change is good, it brings me growth,**
> **It often brings what I need most.**

When the clay becomes soft and pliable, roll it into a ball and smooth it with your fingers. Write your name on it with a pen, then chant:

> **This ball before me, once a cube,**
> **Symbolizes the change I need in attitude.**
> **As I bake it, bake in me**
> **The ease of flexibility.**

Bake the clay according to the package directions. Carry the ball with you until you feel yourself become more flexible, then keep it in a spot where you can look at it frequently.

◆ Spell for Adaptability

To become more adaptable to change, use an opal as a focal point. Watch its colors change and flow, one into the other. Say:

> Opal, stone of varied hue,
> Ease my trial of changes, too.
> As your colors change with ease,
> Free me from rigidity, please.

Carry the opal with you. Repeat the spell when you have difficulty adapting to progress and transitions.

Childbirth

◆ Spell for Easy Childbirth

white candle	6-inch square blue cloth
vegetable oil	yellow ribbon or yarn
powdered lavender	

Work this spell every morning for a week before your delivery date. Anoint the white candle with vegetable oil and roll it in the powdered lavender. Light the candle, and sit or lie down in a comfortable position. Place both hands on your belly, and pray the following prayer:

> Mother Goddess, hold my hand,
> And stay with me throughout this time.
> Cradle me in Your loving arms,
> And talk to me of Nature's rhyme.
> Ease the pains of labor when
> The time comes for this baby's birth;
> Comfort me and guide me through
> Its deliverance onto Earth,
> And grant that labor not be long,
> And that this baby's born with ease,
> And that our lives be filled with laughter.
> Thank you, Mother. Blessed be!

Burn the candle for fifteen minutes every day. On the seventh day, let the candle burn down completely. Place the wick and melted wax (if any) in the center of the cloth and sprinkle with lavender. Mark a pentagram over the cloth with your finger and tie it closed with the ribbon. Keep the pouch with you during labor and delivery.

◆ **Easing Labor Pains**
Burn a mixture made of lavender and sandalwood in the birthing room to ease labor pains and bring a smooth delivery.

―――――――――――――――――――――― **Cleansing**

◆ **To Cleanse Stones and Stones Set in Jewelry**

Though the old-fashioned method of cleansing stones in saltwater works well, the mixture often corrodes metal jewelry settings. Instead, put stones in the freezer for twenty-four hours; this process removes all negative energy and doesn't harm precious metals.

◆ **To Cleanse Crystals and Stones**

Place stones and crystals in a thriving pot of African violets, leaving them there for three days. (**Caution:** Excessively nasty energy could cause the plant to die.)

◆ **To Cleanse the Physical Body**

Add two cups of salt to a full bath. Place your hands over the water and chant:

> **Salt and water purify**
> **Negative energy where it lies.**
> **Cleanse my body tress to toe.**
> **As I will now, make it so!**

Completely immerse yourself several times, being certain to cleanse each bodily orifice with the saltwater. (**Note:** For eyes and nostrils, use a drop or two of water on your fingertips. If you have any cuts, scrapes, or abrasions, you may want to put this bath on hold until you heal. Salt has excellent healing properties, but it does tend to sting raw flesh.)

◆ To Cleanse a Magical Working Space

small bowl or basket	censer
chamomile	equal parts of dragon's blood, frankincense, and myrrh
hematite	box of table salt
charcoal block	

Place the bowl or basket in the center of the working space. Fill it with chamomile and place the hematite on top. Lay your hands over the basket and chant:

> **Stone and flower, now erase**
> **Negative energy in this space.**
> **Force it out and send it down**
> **Into the Earth where it can ground.**

Light the charcoal and place it in the censer. Add the equal parts of dragon's blood, frankincense, and myrrh. Starting at the East and working widdershins, cense the boundaries of the area three times. With every pass, chant:

> **Smoke and Fire of ancient lore**
> **Purify every pore**
> **Of this space and cleanse it free**
> **Of smut and negative energy.**

Place the censer at the East.

Take the box of table salt; starting at the East and working deosil, scatter its contents along the area boundaries. As you scatter the salt, chant:

Evil, you must go away.
All good spirits come and stay.

Stand in the center of the area with your arms stretched outward. Say:

This place be purified and free
Of all matter of negativity.
All work and spells shall flow with ease
As I will, so mote it be!

When the charcoal burns out, bury the ashes in the ground or flush them down the toilet. Place the basket of chamomile and hematite in a prominent area of the space.

◆ To Cleanse Ritual Tools

white candle	small bowl of water
frankincense or sandalwood incense	small dish of soil

Light the candle and the incense. Pass the tool through the incense smoke and chant:

I cleanse you with the breath of Air,
Winds blown cold and winds blown fair.

Pass the tool through the candle flame. Chant:

I cleanse you with the warmth of Fire,
Dancing flame and purifier.

Asperge the tool with water. Chant:

With Water I cleanse and give you life,
Babbling brook and surging knife.

Sprinkle the tool with soil. Chant:

I cleanse you with the depths of Earth,
Home of death and place of birth.

Take the tool in both hands and lift it skyward. Say:

Be free of negativity!
As I will, so mote it be!

Communication

◆ To Have Someone Contact You

new embroidery needle
yellow candle

If you wish to hear from someone, firmly push the needle into the center of an un-anointed yellow candle (Figure 2). When the eye of the needle is flush with the wax, inscribe the person's name on the candle. Concentrate intently on the person contacting you, and

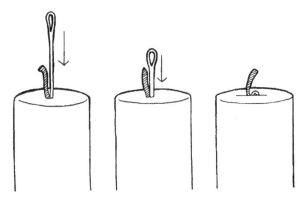

Figure 2.

light the wick. Let the candle burn out. (The person usually calls before the candle burns half-way.)

◆ Salt Spell

This is another great spell to use when you need to contact someone with whom you have lost touch.

Place a glass of water in the center of your working area. Pour two to three tablespoons of salt into your dominant hand and use it to make three equal-armed crosses over the glass, allowing some salt to flow into the water. As you make the salt crosses, chant:

> **Hear me, call me, get in touch.**
> **We need to talk. Please hurry! Rush!**

Expect to hear from the person by the time the water evaporates.

◆ Bay Leaf Spell

To hear from someone by telephone, write his or her name on a bay leaf and tape it to the underside of your phone handset. Chant:

> (Name of person), call me—phone now ring.
> To my ears, (name of person)'s voice now bring.

◆ Charging Communication Stones

After programming stones for communication spells or knowledge retention, place them on top of the computer for charging.

Computers

◆ Protection Against Computer Viruses

Turn the computer on and defragment the hard drive. While the computer sorts its files, thoroughly clean the computer case, monitor, drives, and keyboard of all dust. Chant:

> Mercury, Zeus, Apollo, Thor,
> Protect this fine machine.
> Keep its files where they belong
> And its hardware virus-free.

◆ General Computer Protection

This is a great spell for any computer, but especially for those just entering the home. Follow the directions outlined above, but use this chant instead.

Earth and Wind and Fire and Sea,
Moon and Sun: All hear my plea.
Communications deities
All come forth and present be.
Join in forces and protect
All data, pixels, and connects.
Then weave a web both tight and sound
To stave off crashes this way bound.
Protect my software from all harm
And hardware, too, from raging storm.
Please guard it well from other tricks
Like Loki's jokes and Murphy's kicks.
Stamp out virus and disease
So data flows to me with ease.
To my aid, oh Ancients, come
Protect by Moon and shining Sun.

◆ To Protect Power Flow

To help protect against power interrupts and surges, place a quartz crystal near the electrical outlet used to plug in your computer.

◆ To Keep Loaded Software Running Efficiently

Aces from a Tarot deck (all four)

4 quartz crystals

Place the Aces on top of the central processing unit (CPU) as shown in Figure 3 (following page): the Ace of Pentacles with the Ace of Swords below it, the Ace of Wands to the right of the Ace of Pentacles, and the

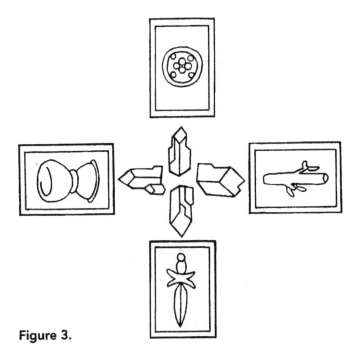

Figure 3.

Ace of Cups to its left. In the center space between the cards, place a crystal with its point toward the center edge of each card.

As you arrange each crystal, say:

> **Give programs energy to work with ease,**
> **So they run smooth and do not freeze.**
> **Bring perfect function from my keys.**
> **As I will, so mote it be!**

Leave the arrangement for a week, and repeat the spell every time you load new software.

Computer Peripherals

◆ Charm to Increase Modem Speed

For speeding modem upload and download time, try placing a piece of tiger-eye on top of external modems. For internal modems, place the stone on top of the CPU. The results are remarkable.

◆ Fax/Modem Protection Chant

Zeus of roaring, rumbling thunder;
Thor of lightning, Fiery Wonder;
Loki, Murphy—tricksters, dear;
Keep your mischief far from here!
Protect, oh Mercury, this device
And keep its uploads clear and nice.
Its downloads send with greatest ease,
And put them where they ought to be.
From bit bucket heaven, please protect
All bytes and pixels I elect
To zip and send across the land—
Carry them safely in Your hand!

◆ Chant for a Properly Functioning CD-ROM

Hera, hearken—hear my plea!
Keep this CD-ROM dust-free.
Muses, come and set the pace,
Let music and .gifs flow from this place.
Sarasvati, let the text flow free.
As I will, so mote it be!

◆ Chant for a Properly Functioning Printer

Mercury of winged foot,
Watch over every key that's pushed,
So that this printer gets the news
And does what it's supposed to do.
Printer, print just what I feed,
Print it clearly—bold and clean.
Grab each pixel and each byte
And print them with the speed of light.

◆ Chant for a Properly Functioning Scanner

Goddess, Brighid—Artsy One—
Let this scanner smoothly run
And copy now with true precision
Each page and word as I envision.
Scanner, memorize each byte
Of pixel, text, of dark and light.
Photograph it clear and true
And feed it to the CPU.

◆ Computer Disk Talisman

The following process places a spell in a strong magnetic field. This helps draw magical goals in your direction and removes the need for further charging.

To create this talisman, type or copy a ritual or spell appropriate to your goal onto the computer hard drive. As you type or copy, see yourself performing the ritual and attaining your goal. Save the ritual, move it to a blank disk, then carry the disk with you.

Consecration

◆ General Consecration for Ritual Tools

(Deity/deities of choice), I ask that You
Add Your power to this tool.
Bless it in Your sacred Name
And never let its power wane.
I consecrate this tool to Thee.
As I will, so mote it be.

Courage

(For related spells, see "Fear.")

◆ Charm for Courage

jewelry item
musk or cedar oil

Obtain a piece of jewelry. Any sort will do as long as
it is something that you like enough to wear frequently. Rub a bit of oil into the piece and chant:

I imbue you with courage, and bravery, and nerve,
I empower you with self-confidence,
so you may serve
My needs when anxieties attempt to emerge
Eradicate them; let new confidence surge.

Wear the jewelry as needed.

◆ Charms to Encourage Self-Confidence

Hematite is the stone of warriors and soldiers. Carry a small piece in your pocket and handle it any time self-confidence wanes.

Chewing catnip promotes courage and self-confidence as well.

Creativity

(For related spells, see "Inspiration.")

◆ Creativity Ritual

salt	small pot of earth
green candle	pencil and paper
olive oil	bowl of water
yellow candle	handful of pinto beans, flower seeds, or other easily sprouting seeds
Creativity incense (see recipe section in chapter three)	1–2 fertilizer sticks
scissors	

Instead of a formal Circle, cast a triple one made of salt. While casting the first Circle, say:

For the Goddess.

On the second pass, say:

For the God.

And on the third, say:

For the Muses.

Stand in the center of the Circle and facing the appropriate directions, informally invite the Elements to join you and lend Their energies. Anoint the green candle with olive oil. Light it and say:

Green is the color of verdant growth.
It nourishes my core.
It brings fertile richness to my life
And makes my spirit soar.

Anoint the yellow candle and light it, saying:

Come to me spirit of the Muse,
Renew my spirit and my soul.
Grant me productivity.
Make me new and whole.

Place a drop of oil on the incense, light it and say:

Fire and herb and smoke and Air,
Fused together well,
Grant your essence unto me
And aid me in this spell.

While concentrating on removing the barrenness from your Creative Self, take the pot of earth and till it well with your fingers, smoothing out every clump until it is as fine as silk. As you smooth the soil, chant over and over:

> **I am the child of the Goddess.**
> **I am the child of the God.**
> **Their energies live within me**
> **And nourish the spiritual sod**
> **That before has laid so dry and cracked—**
> **But now is soft and fine—**
> **And lies ready for the planting**
> **Of the seeds of the Divine.**

When the soil is ready, stop for a few moments and make a list of the problems contributing to your creativity block. Cross out each problem and in a column beside it, write its opposite. For example, if procrastination is one of the problems, tenacity might be a good alternative; lethargy might be replaced with energy, depression with joy, and so on. Complete the list.

Take a bean or seed and plunge it into the bowl of water, saying something like:

> **I cleanse myself of (problem).**
> **I wash it all away.**
> **I replace it now with (opposite),**
> **Which is here to stay.**

Remove the bean or seed from the water and say:

> **You are now the quality of (opposite)**
> **and contain all the elements thereof.**

Plant the bean in the pot of earth. Go through the entire list in the same manner until all the beans have been cleansed and planted. Push the fertilizer sticks into the pot and water the seeds well, saying:

**As I fertilize these seeds,
so is my center nourished.**

Visualize the seeds sprouting and growing into lush and healthy plants. After a few moments, say:

**Grow little seeds, for as you do
Your qualities will grow in me.
Our ground is fertile, our roots grow strong.
As I will, so mote it be!**

Cut the list in half and burn the "problem column" in the incense burner, symbolically removing those blocks forever from your life. Fold the remaining paper several times (nine, if you are able) and "plant" it in the pot. Thank the Elements for Their help and bid Them farewell. Know that the problems are gone and that the core of your existence is fertile again and ready to produce.

(**Note:** Don't forget to water the seeds and transplant them if necessary, for your new qualities will grow as they flourish.)

◆ Charm for a Creative Boost

Keep citrine and orange calcite nearby when you need a creative boost. They are connected to the Muses and do much to aid the creative flow.

Daily Blessings ───────────────

◆ **Morning Blessing**

Shortly after rising, light a white candle and say this
blessing or the alternative one on the next page. I
guarantee that you will see a difference in the quality
of your day.

I call upon You, Sisters Three,
You Who sit beneath Life's Tree,
Bless and watch over me this day.
These things of You, I ask and pray.
Mighty Clothos, You Who spin
The thread and yarn of life on whim,
Grant my thread be soft, yet strong
And the essence of my own life's song
Mighty Lachesis, You Who weave
And measure the cloth of Life with ease,
Weave my life beautifully
With color and texture for all to see.
Mighty Atropos, You Who slice
Life's fabric and thread with a snip precise,
Grant me now another day
To return to thank You—this I pray.
Mighty Ones, oh Sisters Three,
You Who sit beneath the Tree,
For each day I awaken to
Accept the thanks I offer You!

◆ Alternate Morning Blessing

Gracious Creator/rix, Who lives within Me,
Help me to understand Your ways.
Guide my feet as they trod Your path
And keep me safely out of harm's way.
Teach me to trust myself, my inner child,
and my instincts,
For I am a product of Your Creative Force;
And by my very existence
Form an important part of Your Universal Plan.
Make my life not a test,
But instead—a joy
And speak to me through my intuitive nature
So that I cease to see my whims and fancies
As mere frivolity.
Let me view them, instead,
As what they are—
An important part of who I am
In Your world.
So mote it be.

◆ Bedtime Blessing

As I lay snuggled in my bed,
Pillow tucked beneath my head,
Maiden, bring me joyful dreams.
Mother, bring me peace, serene.
Wisest Crone, watch over me.
Until the light of dawn, I see.

And let me wake up safe and sound
Each day that to this Earth, I'm bound.

◆ Before Meal Blessing

Oh Mother Earth, we thank You so
For the food and beverage You bestow,
For Your protection and Your love,
And everything You do for us.
We offer You thanks, love, and mirth
As we eat Your bounty, Mother Earth.

Depression ─────────────

(For related spells, see "Anxiety" and "Stress.")

◆ Depression Relief Spell

white candle (non-dripless variety)	kunzite or blue agate
black marker with wide felt tip	lemon balm
lemon oil (the kind used for furniture polish is fine)	cloth pouch

Begin by completely coloring the candle black with the marker to symbolize the depression that presently encases you. Light the candle and say:

> Flame cut through depression, deep
> Melt it down and make it weep.
> Grant me power to re-emerge,
> From its grip, I leap and surge.

Watch the candle burn until white wax appears at the flame.

Rub a bit of lemon oil into the stone and say:

> Kunzite/agate, stone of mellow hue,
> Dissolve this depression, I beg of you.
> Take its power and transform its strength
> Into positive energy I can use at length.

Lightly rub the stone against your temples and your heart, then place it in front of the candle and sprinkle it with lemon balm. Let the candle burn completely. Place the stone and herb in the cloth pouch and carry it with you. When your spirits need a lift, re-anoint the stone and repeat its empowerment chant.

◆ Blues Eradicator Drink

1 cup lemon balm leaves (fresh, if possible)   plastic wrap

large pitcher   1 bottle ginger ale

1 bottle white wine (Riesling or other fruity type)   lemon slices

or

1 quart lemonade (for an alcohol-free drink)

Bruise the lemon balm and place the leaves in the pitcher. Pour the wine over them and chant:

Wine and herb now mix together,
Bring my spirit sunny weather.
As I sip you, blues be gone
By breeze, Earth, sea, and shining Sun.

Cover the pitcher with plastic wrap and store in the refrigerator for a least one hour. Fill a tall glass with ice, then pour it half full of wine. Finish filling the glass with ginger ale, stir, and garnish with the lemon slice. Hold the glass high in a toast to the deities, and chant:

A happy life, I grant myself—
The joy of faeries, sprites, and elves!
As I sip, depression leave!
As I will, so mote it be!

Sip the drink and feel the blues slip away.

◆ Charm to Dispel Depression

Carry a piece of lotus root on your person to clear the mind of gloomy thoughts and lift the spirits.

Dieting

(For related spells, see "Addiction.")

◆ The Dieting Thought-form Ritual

Take a blue topaz to a quiet place and sit comfortably. Set the stone aside, then close your eyes and hold your hands closely together, palms facing each other. Feel the warmth of energy flow between your fingers and palms. Visualize the energy as a white light.

Move your hands farther apart, forcing the energy stream to broaden. Keep moving your hands and expanding the energy force until you reach a distance of about six inches. Shape the energy into a ball with your fingers, then squeeze and compress it until it is the size of the stone.

Hold the compressed energy in one hand and the topaz in the other, then clasp your hands together to combine the two. Say:

> **Thought form of my energy**
> **In this stone, now live and be.**

Open your hands and breathe on the stone. Say:

> **I share with you my Air to breathe.**

Hold the stone to your forehead, then hold it to your heart. Say:

> **I give you the Fires of passion and intellect.**

Rub some saliva into the stone. Say:

I give you the Waters of Life.

Rub the stone across your feet. Say:

I give you the strength of foundation.

Hold the stone in your dominant hand until it tingles and pulses with energy. Open your hand and chant over the stone:

Stone of topaz, bluest stone,
Your life is mine, and mine alone.
Work to curb my appetite
And bring good health back into sight.
Give me strength to stay away
From foods where fat and sugar play.
Bring the will power that I need
As I will, so mote it be!

Wear or carry the stone with you while dieting.

Divination

◆ To Encourage Psychic Abilities

If you are prone to divination difficulties, try sipping a cup of hazelnut coffee or Psychic Tea (see "Psychic Ability" for recipe) before you begin.

To Ease Divination
For ease in divination, store an amethyst with your divination tools and keep one nearby when you read.

◆ Chant for Reading Tarot Cards
This chant is very effective when said before the first card is turned up.

Wisest Ashtaroth, please send
Your guidance and Your wisdom lend.
Help me read with clarity
And speak the truth—so mote it be!

◆ Chant for Reading Runes

Mighty Odin, Runic Keeper,
Guide my mind and be my teacher.
Grant Your wisdom that I may see
The message that is meant to be.

◆ Chant for Scrying

Crone of Wisdom and Dark Skies,
Let the shapes materialize.
Show me clearly what's to come.
As I will, so be it done!

Divorce ——————————————

(For related spells, see the sections on "Heartbreak" and "Peaceful Separation.")

◆ Ritual for Easing the Pain of Divorce

photograph of you and your former mate	white candle
matches	small bunch of violets (substitute a few stalks of lavender or a white rose if you like)
fireproof dish half full of soil	bowl of water

Hold the photograph and look at it carefully. Memorize every detail. When you can see it clearly in your mind, light a match and set the picture aflame, beginning with a corner that pictures your former mate. Place it in the dish and as it burns, say:

We once had love where now is grief.
I give your life back and relieve
You of all power over me.
My life is mine—I set me free!

Dip the flowers in the water and use them to asperge your body from head to toe. Say:

I wash grief away with water clear.
I wash and cleanse myself of fear.
And as I wash, I gain new power.
I am reborn this very hour.

Write your name on the candle and light it. Watch as the flame gains life and grows strong. Say:

I accept this brand new life
And free myself from stress and strife,
And guilt and pain and misery
As I will, so mote it be!

Let the candle burn completely.

◆ Charm to Ease the Pain of Divorce

Bittersweet or lemon balm placed under the pillow eases the pain of divorce and brings the fresh perspective necessary to start life anew.

Dreams

◆ Prophetic Dream Tea

1 teaspoon chamomile	2 teaspoons rose petals
½ teaspoon cinnamon	1 teaspoon peppermint
1 teaspoon mugwort	

Mix the ingredients well. Use one teaspoon of tea for every cup of boiling water. As the tea steeps, chant:

Tea of vision, dreaming tea,
As I sip you, bring to me
An altered state conducive to
Psychic dreams. And when I'm through,
Rock me gently into sleep
And bring the answers that I need.

Sweeten with honey, if desired. Drink the tea thirty minutes before going to bed.

Store the dry tea in a plastic bag with a zipper closure or in a glass jar with a tight-fitting lid.

◆ Dream Pouch

anise seed	mugwort
chamomile	rosemary
cloves	rose petals
mint	small cloth pouch

Mix bits of the herbs together until you have a scent to your liking. Stuff the cloth pouch with the mixture, and charge it by chanting:

Psychic dream mix, come alive!
Mingled energies now thrive.
Show me what I need to see
As I sleep. So mote it be!

Place the pouch inside your pillowcase. Replace the mixture in the pouch when the scent dissipates. Store the formula in a plastic bag with a zipper closure.

◆ To Dream of Past Lives

Wearing an opal to bed or sleeping with one under your pillow works well for inducing dreams of prior incarnations.

◆ To Recall Dream

To remember dreams, place red jasper on your headboard or nightstand before falling asleep.

◆ To Dream of True Love

Tuck five bay leaves in your pillow case on Valentine's Day to bring dreams of your true love.

─────────── Eloquence

◆ Spell for Effective Speaking

This spell is excellent for those who stutter or cannot seem to effectively verbalize their thoughts.

sprig of fresh thyme   carnelian

or

¼ teaspoon dried thyme
soaked overnight in
1 tablespoon vegetable oil

Rub the thyme between your thumb and index finger until its scent remains on them. (If you opted for the oil, put a drop on your index finger.) Rub the thyme scent or the oil into the carnelian, then use the stone to mark a pentagram each on your forehead, lips, and throat. Hold the stone and visualize yellow light streaming into it from your Third Eye. Chant:

Sarasvati, One Who Flows,
Bring an end to speaking woes.
Let my thoughts roll off my tongue
With eloquence in Moon or Sun.
Let them flow with perfect ease.
Bring me perfect diction, please.
All babbling ramble, now purloin.
Make my words connect and join,
So I can make my point with ease.
As I will, so mote it be!

Carry the stone with you, and rub it whenever you experience speaking difficulties. As you rub it, silently pray the first two lines of the chant to Sarasvati:

Sarasvati, One Who Flows,
Bring an end to speaking woes.

◆ To Promote Language and Speaking Skills

A charm bag filled with slippery elm and worn around the neck promotes good language and speaking skills.

Empathy

(For related spells, see "Apathy.")

◆ Prayer to Become More Empathetic

Goddess Mother of compassion,
Help me now to understand
How others feel, so I can help them.
Guide me with Your gentle hand.
Bring to me their true emotions,
Bring their dreams, their hopes, their fears,
Bring their hurts, that I may soothe them,
Bring their laughter and their tears.
Help me be more empathetic
To the needs of others, please,
And help me nurture all around me.
As I will, so mote it be!

◆ To Remove the Negative Energy Picked Up From Others

Empaths often have difficulty letting go of the emotional garbage and pain they draw from others. Left unchecked, these left-leftovers can cause anxiety and physical illness.

To remove the overflow, visualize a tiny hole in the small of your back. Mentally move the negative energy down toward the hole and let it seep out into the Earth. When no more negative energy remains, close the hole.

Enemies

◆ **To Stop Someone from Interfering in Your Life**

Write the name of your enemy on a piece of paper
and place it in a plastic bag with a zipper closure. Fill
the bag three-fourths full of water, zip it shut, and
put it in your freezer.

◆ **To Make Someone Leave You Alone**

Anoint a handkerchief or small doily with patchouli
oil, while saying:

> (Name of person) go away.
> Out of my life forever stay.

Mail it to the person in question. Do not put a return
address on the envelope.

Energy

◆ **Stone Charm for Physical Energy**

Take a piece of sunstone to an eastern windowsill at
sunrise. (Alternatively, place the stone outside in the
East where it can absorb the rays of the morning Sun.)
Offer the stone to the Sun and chant:

> Flaming Orb of rising power
> Add vital energy hour by hour
> To this stone with flecks of gold
> Give it Your power, great and bold,
> And when the light of day is through

> And with Your zest this stone is imbued,
> It shall come back home to me
> To impart Your zestful energy.

Leave the stone to absorb the energy of the rising Sun, but don't retrieve it until after sundown. (This gives the energy time to "settle" in the stone.) Carry it with you.

Fear

(For related spells, see "Courage.")

◆ Charm to Promote Fearlessness

purple candle	4-inch square purple fabric
Mars incense (optional; see recipe section in chapter three)	3 pinches dragon's blood powder
bloodstone or hematite	red ribbon or yarn

Light the candle and incense, and meditate a few moments on your reasons for fear. Examine them closely and rid yourself of any born of less than solid reasoning.

Place the stone on the cloth and say:

> Bloodstone/hematite, Warrior's Stone,
> Grant that fear no longer roam
> Inside my heart or in my head.
> Crush it, stone—it's gone and dead.

Sprinkle the dragon's blood powder over the stone one pinch at a time. With the first pinch, say:

With this pinch, my fear dilute.
Reduce its voice until it's mute.

With the second pinch, say:

The second chases fear away
And dissolves it so it cannot stray.

And with the third, say:

The third one brings me nerves of steel
And helps me face each new ordeal.

Gather the fabric edges together and secure with the ribbon to form a pouch. Place the pouch in front of the candle. Leave it there until the candle burns out, then carry the bag with you.

◆ Fear Alleviating Spell

pen and paper

Mars incense (see recipe section in chapter three)

List all your fears on a piece of paper, then rip the paper to shreds. Place the pieces in a fireproof dish, sprinkle the incense on top, and light. Flush the ashes down the toilet.

◆ Chant to Alleviate Fear

Kali, Destroyer, Fearsome One,
Help me now to overcome
This fear that has a hold on me
And drown it in Your Bloody Sea.
Consume this demon known as Fright,
Protect me with Your awesome might.
Lend Your strength and help me face
Whatever comes into my space.
Aid me now, oh Ancient One.
As I will, so be it done!

◆ To Find the Source of Fear

It is often difficult to control or eliminate fear unless we know its underlying causes. To find the source of fear, wear or carry leopardskin jasper. Its energies cut through fear's defensive wrappings and allow the real problem to surface.

Fertility

◆ Tree Spell

pen and paper   water
9 fertilizer spikes

Write your request for fertility on a piece of paper. (**Note**: It is important to be specific when stating your request. Non-specifics can result in pregnancy or fertilization of other areas you might rather leave alone.) Wrap a fertilizer spike in the paper, and plant it at the eastern-most base of a tree. As you cover the hole with dirt, chant:

> **I fertilize you now, my friend,**
> **Giving barrenness a speedy end.**
> **As you feed upon this spike,**
> **Send my request with power and might.**
> **Bring what I ask straight back to me—**
> **Lush abundance and fertility.**

Working clockwise, push the rest of the spikes into the soil around the tree, saying with each one:

> **Abundance, plenty, fertility come!**
> **As you feed, the deed is done.**

Water the tree, give it a hug, and thank it for its help.

Focus

◆ Spell to Gain Focus

> white candle   magnifying glass
> vanilla extract   pencil and paper

Draw an eye on the candle. Place a few drops of vanilla extract on the candle top, and work a little into the wick. Pay attention to the aroma and inhale it deeply. Light the candle and say:

Quiet, mind, now be still.
Focus on what I now will.
No scattering or thought dissension—
I order you to pay attention.

Hold the magnifying glass in front of the eye on
the candle, then bring it up to your Third Eye. Say:

Bring clear focus to details
Enlarge and bring them into scale
Attend each project one by one
Grant clarity 'til work is done

Make a to-do list in order of priority and place it
in front of the candle. Put the magnifying glass on
top of the list. Leave them there until the candle
burns completely. Then carry the glass with you, and
get started on the list.

◆ **To Promote Concentration**
Burn a mixture of sandalwood and celery seed to promote deep concentration and sharp focus.

Forgiveness ──────────────────────

◆ Spell to Gain Forgiveness from Another

1 ice cream bar stick   sugar

pen   water

quart jar with screw-on lid

Write the name of the offended person on one side of the stick and your name on the other side. Place the stick in the jar. Fill the jar half full with sugar. Chant:

> **In this sugar, we both stand**
> **Back to back, but hand to hand.**
> **Change (name of other person)'s**
> **sour thoughts of me**
> **To sweet forgiving thoughts, I plead.**

Add water until the jar is three-fourths full. Say:

> **With this water, I wash away**
> **All that keeps us now at bay.**
> **Sugar water, I now pray**
> **Let forgiveness come my way.**

Cap the jar tightly and shake it nine times, saying:

> **Sugar syrup, do your thing**
> **And (name of other person)'s**
> **forgiveness, quickly bring.**
> **Soak him/her in thoughts of me so sweet**
> **That his/her forgiveness is complete.**

Shake the jar nine times each day while saying the last chant.

◆ Spell to Become More Forgiving

> 1 bunch of fresh parsley   bowl of water
> white ribbon or yarn

Tie the parsley into a bunch, securing it with the ribbon. Dip the leaves in the water and asperge yourself thoroughly with them, saying:

> **I wash away all hurt and pain,**
> **I wash away scorn and disdain.**
> **All contempt I hereby purge.**
> **Let sweet forgiveness now emerge.**

Hang the parsley over your bed to complete its magic while you sleep.

Friendship

◆ To Become Open to New Relationships

> pink candle   sunflower oil
> rose quartz

Inscribe a pink candle with your name, then anoint it and the rose quartz with sunflower oil. Light the candle. Hold the stone in your hand, and visualize friendships coming your way and new relationships forming.

Chant three times:

> Open mind, and gain new life,
> Gone from you, all stress and strife.
> Open heart, gain life anew,
> Accept all love that's offered you.
> Positive thought and word and deed
> Enter now—of bane I'm freed.
> Ancients, hear me—grant my plea
> To new relationships, open me.

Place the stone by the candle and leave it there until the candle burns all the way down. Carry the stone with you.

◆ To Attract Others of a Like Mind

orange candle	needle and thread
vanilla oil	6 sunflower seeds (soaked overnight in water to soften the outer shells)

Anoint the candle with vanilla oil and light it. As it burns, chant:

> Come from here and come from there
> People whom my ideals share.
> Come one, come now, come all to me
> By Sun, Wind, Earth, and Shining Sea!

Thread the needle and string through the first sunflower seed. Say:

> With seed one, the spell's begun.

String the second seed, saying:

With seed two, my wish comes true.

With the third:

With seed three, it comes to me.

Fourth:

With seed four, it's at my door.

Fifth:

With seed five, it grows and thrives.

And with the sixth seed:

With seed six, the spell is fixed.

Knot the ends of the thread together to form a ring. Rub a little vanilla oil into the seed ring, and leave it by the candle until it burns out. Carry the ring with you as an attraction charm.

◆ To Gain New Friends

After sunrise on three consecutive Sunday mornings, face East and chant:

Apollo, Ra, and Gods of Sun,
Sun Goddesses and Ancient Ones,
Hearken, hearken, hear my plea
With friendship, bless and shower me!

◆ To Maintain Friendship

3 lengths of white embroidery floss

3 lengths of embroidery floss in your friend's favorite color

3 lengths of embroidery floss in your favorite color

To find the proper floss length, wrap the floss around your wrist twice, then add and extra eight inches.

Knot all nine lengths of floss together, leaving a four-inch tail. Using all three lengths of each color as one strand, braid the lengths together (Figure 4).

While you braid, chant:

(Your name), (friend's name), and Maiden One,

I bind you now in joy and fun.

Braid and chant until the piece is 7½ inches long. Knot the ends and leave a 4-inch tail. Tie the bracelet around your friend's wrist.

Figure 4.

Gambling

◆ Spell for Gambling Luck

green candle	1 nickel
yellow candle	1 dime
magnetic oil (vegetable oil in which a magnet has soaked for 3 days)	1 quarter
1 dollar bill	½ teaspoon chamomile
1 penny	orange ribbon or yarn

Draw a dollar sign on the green candle, an arrow pointing to the right on the orange candle, and an arrow pointing to the left on the yellow candle (Figure 5).

Figure 5.

Anoint the candles with the magnetic oil. Place the green candle in the center, the yellow candle on its right, and the orange candle on its left. Light the green candle and say:

> **Money come and money grow.**
> **Money green, to me now flow.**

Light the orange candle and say:

> **Like a magnet, draw luck and money.**
> **It flows to me like milk and honey.**

Light the yellow candle and say:

> **Success come wrap your spell around**
> **My gambling luck and make it sound**

Place the dollar bill in front of the candles. Put a few drops of magnetic oil on the index finger of your dominant hand. Trace a diagonal line with your finger from the upper right-hand corner of the bill to its lower left-hand corner; then trace a line from the lower right-hand corner to the upper left-hand corner to form an X. Say:

> **With crossing magnet, I seal this bill.**
> **Bring others 'til my pockets fill.**

Place the penny in the middle of the bill and say:

> **A penny for luck.**

Put the nickel on top of it, saying:

A nickel to build.

Place the dime on top of the nickel, saying:

A dime for cash flow.

Top the coins with the quarter, saying:

A quarter to seal.

Sprinkle the chamomile on top of the coins and say:

Success and fortune in this bill.
So mote it be, just as I will!

Fold the long sides of the bill over the coins, and fold the short ends toward the center to form a packet. Wind the ribbon or yarn around the packet nine times, saying:

What I wish, now bring to me.
As I will, so mote it be!

Secure the binding with a knot. Place the packet in front of the green candle and leave it there until the candles burn down. Carry the gambling charm with your pocket money.

◆ For Good Luck in Gambling
Carry a pair of buckeyes or three tiger-eye stones with your pocket change to increase gambling luck.

◆ For Luck with Cards

Washing the hands in chamomile tea is said to bring luck to those who gamble with cards.

Gardening━━━━━━━━━━━━━━━━

◆ Spell to Bless a Spring Garden

1 quart milk	garden seeds or plants
½ cup honey	2 stakes or sticks for each garden row
2-quart container	pastel ribbons (one for each stake)
small tree or bush branch with newly sprouted leaves and buds	

Take all the materials outside to the garden. Mix the milk and honey together and pour it into the container. Place the branch in the container and set aside.

Poke a stake in the ground at the beginning and end of each row, then sow the seeds and/or set the plants. Tie a ribbon bow around each stake, saying to the seeds and plants in that row:

Perfect love, I give to you.
Sprout and thrive with life anew.

Pick up the container and using the branch, asperge the garden with milk and honey. Consecrate it, saying:

Milk and honey, flow throughout,
Fertilize each seed and sprout.
Maiden, Green Man, dance and play,
Twirl and laugh here every day.
Bring lush growth and green this spot
Everywhere you skip and walk.

Water the garden thoroughly. Tend to its needs daily.

◆ Spell for Planting Fall Bulbs

Take the bulbs to the garden and place them in the earth, chanting:

Seasons change—the Wheel turns 'round!
Bulbs, I plant you in the ground.
Death-like bulbs, you'll gain new life,
And in the Spring, will sprout and thrive.

As you cover them with soil, chant:

Maiden Goddess, dance and play
Upon this ground throughout the day.
Wisest Crone, so gnarled and old,
Work mysteries in the night-time cold.
Mother Goddess, give them birth
So they will sprout upon the Earth.
And let them blossom beauteously.
The Wheel turns 'round! So mote it be!

Water them well, and repeat the previous chant once a day until the first bulb sprouts.

◆ To Promote Growth

"Plant" clear quartz crystals or moss agate in the center of any type of garden to promote lush growth and abundant harvest.

◆ To Protect the Garden from Animals

To keep rabbits and other animals from eating the fruits of your labor, stuff pieces of old pantyhose with human hair. As you stuff, chant:

> **Deter all wildlife from this place**
> **So that this garden thrives in grace.**

Knot the pieces at both ends to form pouches and lay them at the corners of the garden. Vegetable-seeking animals will not cross into the area.

◆ Using Lunar Energy for Magical Gardens

Between dark Moon and waxing Moon, plant crops that reach above the ground and re-seed themselves.

If they reach above the ground and have seed pods, plant them between waxing Moon and full Moon.

If they grow below the ground (root crops, bulbs), plant them between full Moon and waning Moon.

Use the period between waning Moon and dark Moon to weed and harvest.

━━━━━━━━━━━━━━━━━━━━━━━━━━ **Goals**

◆ **Plant Spell**

pen and paper	1 packet flower seeds *or* a small flowering plant that isn't blooming yet
flower pot and potting soil	1 fertilizer spike
green candle anointed with vegetable oil	

Write your goal on the paper. Fill the pot half full of soil, then light the candle and say:

> **Candle, green, of fertile hue,**
> **With growth and power, I imbue.**

Pass the seed packet through the flame three times and say:

> **Seeds/Plant, now dormant, ease my pain.**
> **By spell, this goal help me attain.**

(If you opted for the plant, pass the candle deosil around the plant three times, then say the chant.)

Pass the fertilizer spike through the flame three times and say:

> **Fertilizer stick so rich**
> **Grow this spell without a hitch.**

Place the paper in the pot. Say:

> **Goal I place on fertile earth**
> **Grow in value and in worth.**

Cover the paper with soil until the pot is filled. As you fill the pot, say:

> **Goal, take root now in this soil.**
> **Achievement come with little toil.**

Plant the seeds or plant in the pot, insert the fertilizer stick, and add water, saying:

> **As you bud and grow and sprout/thrive,**
> **Goal achievement blooms**
> **throughout/comes to life.**
> **When you bloom successfully,**
> **My goal's achieved—so mote it be!**

Water and care for the plant while you work toward your goal.

◆ Incense Spell

pen and paper   Success incense (see recipe
                 section in chapter three)

fireproof dish

Write your goal on a piece of paper and put it in the dish. Sprinkle with the incense and light the paper.

As it burns, concentrate on your goal coming to fruition and say:

> Smoke into the Cosmos go
> So the Ancients will now know
> I need assistance to achieve
> This goal that I have set for me.

Repeat this spell every day for a week while working toward your goal.

────────────────────────────── **Gossip**

◆ **Gossip-Stopping Poppet Charm**

black felt	purple embroidery floss
needle and thread	box
cotton or polyester stuffing	newspaper
1 tablespoon slippery elm	

Using the black felt, needle, thread, and stuffing, make a simple poppet (such as the one shown in Figure 6) to represent the offender.

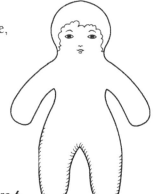

Figure 6.

Cut a slit into the fabric for a mouth and stuff it well with slippery elm. Sew the mouth shut with a six-stranded piece of purple embroidery floss. As you sew, chant:

> **Your mouth is closed. You cannot speak**
> **To gossip, slander, or havoc wreak.**
> **Your mouth stay shut, but only 'til**
> **It speaks of friendship and good will.**

Place the poppet in a box. Stuff the box with paper to force the poppet's face into a corner. Leaving the poppet as such removes the offender's urge to gossip.

◆ To Stop Gossip
Rub deerstongue herb on the soles of your shoes to keep others from speaking ill of you.

Grounding

◆ Exercise 1
Try this exercise when you have trouble settling down.

Sit on the floor and inhale deeply through your nose. Draw in the green energy of the Earth. Exhale fully, expelling the red energy of activity back into the Earth. Repeat three to five times, or until you relax.

◆ Exercise 2
Sit or lie down in a comfortable position and close your eyes. Visualize yourself as a seed beneath the Earth.

Watch as you undergo the germination process. See your roots begin to form below and tiny leaves push forth on top. Watch as your leaves crest the surface and grow toward the Sun. Dig your roots deep into the soil. Stretch and open your eyes.

◆ Grounding Charm

Carry a piece of copper with you and handle it whenever your energies begin to scatter.

Habits

◆ Bad Habit Eradicating Spell

"Take Back My Life" incense (see recipe section in chapter three)

black candle

fireproof dish

"Take Back My Life" oil (vegetable oil may be substituted)

pen and paper

Perform this spell during the waning Moon. Put the incense in the fireproof dish and light the incense. Make a list of all your bad habits, then inscribe symbols of those habits on the candle. Anoint the candle with the oil and roll it in some incense. Then light the candle and say:

Habits, melt just like this wax.
Begone from me right now—make tracks.

Tear the list into little pieces and toss them a few at a time into the incense fire. As they burn, say:

> **Begone bad habits; with Fire I purge**
> **You from my life—you can't emerge.**
> **Reduce to ashes, then to dust.**
> **I take your power. Leave! You must!**

When the paper reduces to ashes, scatter them on the winds, tossing them East, South, West, and North.

◆ To Keep Bad Habits at Bay

Carrying a sage leaf on your person is said to prevent bad habits from returning to you.

Handfasting/Wedding——————

(For related spells, see "Love.")

◆ Chant to Bless the Bride and Groom

> **Bless the fertile soil below.**
> **Bless the plow that tends the row.**
> **Bless the seeds and fruit and flower**
> **And blessings on this new life shower.**
> **Bless the bride and groom today**
> **And bless their love that it might stay.**
> **Bless their children and their bed.**
> **Bless their lives—the newly wed.**

◆ Charm for a Happy Marriage

6 stalks fresh lavender   1 yard pink ribbon

1 rubber band   1 yard burgundy ribbon

Note: If you substitute dried lavender stalks for the fresh ones, soak them in a sink full of cold water for three hours before making this charm.

Tap the stalks on a flat surface to even their ends. Secure the ends with the rubber band, then braid the stalks using two stalks per braiding strand (Figure 7).

As you braid, chant:

Protect and bless this happy life,
The newly wedded: husband and wife.

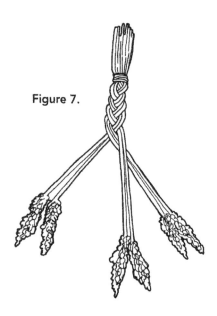

Figure 7.

When you get close to the flower heads, hold the ribbons together and fold them in half to find the center. Center the ribbons under the flower heads and tie the braid securely (Figure 8). Criss-cross the ribbons around the braid working toward the ends. As you wrap with the ribbon, say:

> **Two lives unite and pair as one.**
> **Bring them joy 'til life is done.**

Tie the ribbons in a bow near the stalk ends (Figure 9).Present the charm to the new couple and ask them to hang it over their bed.

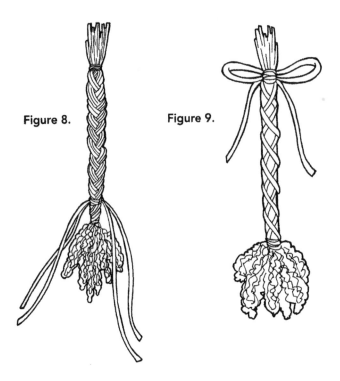

Figure 8.   **Figure 9.**

◆ For a Peaceful Relationship

Place a magnolia leaf under the mattress to ensure a peaceful union.

◆ For a Happy, Loving Relationship

To keep a relationship happy and loving, acquire a pair of Adam and Eve roots and carry them on a constant basis. The feminine partner carries the Adam root and the masculine partner carries the Eve root.

Harmony

◆ Ribbon Spell

soft, gentle music (I like to use classical music for this spell, but any type that soothes you is fine.)	scissors
10 2-yard lengths ¼-inch ribbon (any soft colors will do as long as they don't clash with each other)	1 stick (approximately 6-inches long)

Turn on the music and let its gentle sounds relax you. Then fold one ribbon in half and place the stick on top perpendicular to the ribbon. Bring the ribbon ends over the stick and through the loop (ribbon fold) to form a larkshead knot (Figures 10 and 11, following page).

Pull the ends to tighten. Larkshead each ribbon onto the stick in the same fashion, while chanting:

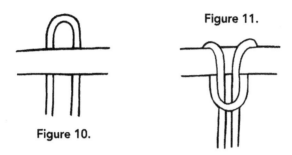

Figure 11.

Figure 10.

**By Earth, dissension is now bound.
Harmony sprouts by knot and sound.**

Working from the left, gather the first four strands in your hand. Using the two outer strands, tie a square knot around the inner two (Figures 12 through 15).

As you work the knot, say:

**Colors weave in harmony,
Knots hold chaos mightily.**

Continue to chant and tie the groups of four until you have a row of five knots.

Working again from the left, push the two outer strands aside and gather the next four strands together. Tie a square knot and chant as before. Continue to knot and chant until you have four knots.

Push the outer four strands aside. Knot and chant until you have three knots. Finally, tie a square knot with the four strands in the center while saying the chant (Figure 16).

Figure 12.

Figure 13.

Figure 14.

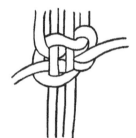

Figure 15.

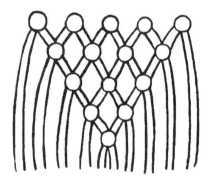

Figure 16.

Trim the ends evenly and hang the piece on a wall in a central location. Chant:

Harmony stay in this place.
Let chaos never show its face.
Keep it bound and grant your peace.
As I will, so mote it be!

◆ Breathing Exercises for Inner and Outer Harmony

For best results, do these exercises in sets of four. Practice them in the morning, at noon, and just before you go to bed at night.

Sit in a comfortable position and straighten your spine. Press the left nostril closed with your finger and inhale with the other until you reach the count of four. Hold the breath for a count of sixteen, then close the right nostril and exhale for a count of eight. Repeat the exercise beginning with the right nostril.

As you breathe, feel the life force and its benefits entering your body. Feel its current move through your body, cleansing, regenerating, strengthening, and energizing. Feel its power clearing your body and spirit of all negative vibrations.

Health and Healing

◆ A Spell for Healing

Light a blue candle and visualize the person who needs healing. When the picture is clear in your mind, target the area of disease and color it bright red. Now visualize tiny workers with buckets of soft green paint, brushes, and rollers. Hold the picture until the workers completely cover the affected area with green. Then open your eyes and chant:

I hold you in my heart
And wrap you in my love.
My circle of protection
Descends now from above.
And as I send this energy,
All pain shall disappear
And all disease shall dissipate
And shrivel up in fear.
The emptiness I now replace
With fresh vitality,
So you may thrive upon the Earth
In laughter, love, and glee.
Brightest blessings and good health, my friend,
Encase you from now on.
I ask that They watch over you
And keep you well and strong.

Let the candle burn all the way out.

◆ Chant for Health and Personal Wellbeing

When said daily, this chant protects against illness.

> Rich health, tranquillity, good energy flow—
> These I conjure to be mine.
> Strength and peace and quietude
> Until the end of time,
> Fluid motion to my joints,
> And clarity of mind.
> Strength to bones and flex to muscles
> I claim these, too, as mine.
> Energy—unboundless force,
> Alertness to my brain,
> Endless inspiration flow
> Where no ideas have lain,
> Great knowledge of my Higher Self,
> And balance to my life,
> I claim these, too, to be my own
> As Sun and Moon both shine.

◆ Apple Seed Health Charm

According to folklore, wearing asafoetida around the neck keeps mental and physical illness away. This comes as no surprise, for the smell is so nasty that nothing can bear to be near it.

Instead, string an even number of apple seeds to wear as a healing necklace. Soak the seeds for eight to ten hours in cold water to soften them. Then thread a sharp needle with monofilament or strong thread and pierce the seeds with the needle to string them.

Charge the necklace by chanting:

Fruit of life and fruit of death,
Hearken to my plea.
Bring good health from both your worlds.
As I will, so mote it be!

◆ To Speed Healing

Hematite is a self-healing stone; scratches on the stone disappear when rubbed with the fingers. To speed personal healing, wear or carry a hematite empowered with the following chant:

Stone of healing, stone of might,
Heal me with the speed of light.

◆ Timing Surgery

Schedule impending surgery during the waning Moon. The Moon's energies control body tides, and excessive bleeding is less likely during this phase.

The following remedies suggest quick fixes for minor problems. They do not alleviate the need for proper medical attention in cases of a serious nature. If these remedies don't resolve the problem immediately, consult your physician.

◆ To Stop Diarrhea

Add one tablespoon nutmeg to one cup of boiling water. Let steep for five minutes, strain, and drink.

◆ To Stop Minor Bleeding

Press a bruised plantain leaf on the wound. The leaf's styptic properties stop minor bleeding immediately.

◆ To Draw Out Insect Venom or Bring Boils to a Head

Add half a cup comfrey leaves to two cups boiling water. Strain through cheesecloth or a 4-inch by 4-inch gauze bandage. Discard the liquid and use the leaves as a hot compress. This works especially well for spider bites.

◆ To Bring Menses

Make a tea of one teaspoon shepherd's purse and one cup of boiling water. Drink one cup of the tea three times daily.

◆ To Counteract Anemia

Eat one cup of blackberries twice daily.

◆ To Soothe and Dry Up Poison Ivy Blisters

Bruise one cup of nasturtium flowers and leaves and tie them in a washcloth. Put the bundle in the bathtub and draw a warm bath. Scrub affected areas with the bundle.

◆ To Soothe Minor Arthritis

Wear copper on a part of the body as close to the affected area as possible.

Heartbreak

(For related spells, see "Divorce.")

◆ Heartbreak Relief Potpourri Spell

bowl	11 drops strawberry oil
1 tablespoon dried yarrow	6 apple seeds
1 tablespoon dried jasmine	1 penny
1 tablespoon dried honeysuckle	quartz crystal
11 drops peach oil	rose quartz

Place the dried herbs in the bowl and add the oils. Place an apple seed at each of the four directions, beginning with East and ending with North. Place the two remaining seeds in the center. Place the penny on top of the center seeds, the clear quartz above it, and the rose quartz below it (Figure 17, page 172).

Then mix the ingredients thoroughly with your hands, and chant:

> Gifts of Earth, sweet potpourri,
> Make heartbreak lift its hold on me,
> As your scent flows 'round about,
> Cast all sadness in me out.
> Herbs, stone, oils, all hear my plea—
> As I will, so mote it be!

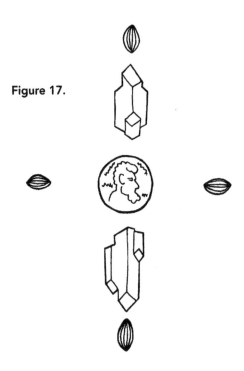

Figure 17.

If there is any oil residue from the potpourri, rub it on your heart. Place the bowl in your bedroom so its scent is the last thing you smell at night and the first thing you smell in the morning.

◆ Charm to Ease a Broken Heart

1 teaspoon honeysuckle	6-inch square yellow cloth
1 teaspoon cyclamen	orange calcite
1 teaspoon lemon balm	lavender ribbon or yarn

On Sunday, mix the herbs and flowers together and place them in the center of the cloth. As you add the herbs, chant:

> **Herbs of sweetness, herbs that soothe,**
> **I ask you now, this grief remove.**
> **Bring to me new peace and joy**
> **And all the sweetness you employ.**

Add the orange calcite and say:

> **Sunny stone that amplifies,**
> **Mix with these herbs and magnify**
> **The goodness of their properties**
> **And grant to me new peace and ease.**

Gather the cloth edges together to form a pouch. Secure the pouch with the ribbon and carry it on your person.

Home

◆ Spell to Own the Home You Want

white candle	salt
red candle	a taglock each from the inside and outside property of the house
vegetable oil	personal taglock (such as a bit of your hair or a fingernail)
Wishing incense (see recipe section in chapter three)	1 penny
pen	rosemary (if you are female)
small white box (a cup box covered with white paper works well)	St. John's wort (if you are male)
water	

First, find the home you want to own. Obtain a taglock from the inside perimeter. Nearly anything will work—a bit of carpet fiber, a paint chip, a shred of wallpaper, dust from the floor—as long as it comes from inside the house. Obtain a taglock from the outside property, too. A blade of grass, a small stone, or a twig is fine.

Take the items home and gather the materials. Light the white candle and summon good spirits and positive influences by chanting something like:

> **Good spirits arise! Be present, please;**
> **Lend this spell your expertise.**

Anoint the red candle with vegetable oil, then roll it in a bit of Wishing incense. This candle represents the heart of the home you want. Light it and chant:

> **Heart of home, I bond with you.**
> **We are one—no longer two.**
> **I am yours and you are mine.**
> **Come to me and waste no time.**

Light the incense. Write your name on all four sides of the box; then open it, and hold it in your hands. Swish it through the incense smoke, and pass it over the flame of the white candle. Place a few drops of water and a pinch of salt inside. Say the following:

> **By fin and feather, scale and fur,**
> **Dwelling changes now occur.**
> **Bring me the home I want to own,**
> **Let no related problems roam.**

Place the house taglocks inside the box and say:

> **I offer you this bit of home**
> **And property to make my own.**

Place your personal taglock inside and say:

> **I offer, too, a bit of me**
> **So that a bond between us be.**

Place the penny inside and say:

> **Money problems shall not come**
> **Between us now. So be it done!**

Sprinkle the inside of the box with the herb appropriate to your gender. Close the box and seal all seams and edges with wax dripped from the red candle. When completely sealed, set the box between the candles and say:

> **Bring this home into my possession**
> **Quickly, now, and without question.**
> **It is mine, so bring it soon.**
> **I claim this space by Sun and Moon.**

Let the candles burn completely.

When the house becomes yours, bury the box as near to the front door as possible.

◆ Home Blessing

If possible, perform this ritual before you move any personal items into a house. (This has nothing to do with the effectiveness of the ritual. It is just easier to do the blessing without furniture and personal belongings in the way.)

> sandalwood incense   dish of water
> white candle   salt shaker filled with salt

Gather the materials and place them in the center of the house. Take the incense to the front east wall of the house and light it, saying:

> **Air with smoke now blow away**
> **Unpleasant energy from this place.**

Travel along every wall in the house, and say the chant with each room you enter. Leave the incense in the center room.

Proceeding as described above, take the candle to the front south wall. Light the candle and say:

> **Candle flame that flickers bright,**
> **Burn negative energy with your light.**

Take the dish of water to the west wall. Sprinkle the water along the walls and chant:

> **Water wash this house and clean**
> **Away all dirt and negativity.**

Take the salt shaker to the north wall. Sprinkle the salt and say:

> **Salt of Earth, both fertile and pure,**
> **Against negative energy, this house secure.**

Stand in the center of the house, spread your legs slightly and open your arms as if to embrace the sky. As you do, chant:

> **God/dess of the home and hearth,**
> **Bless these walls and give them warmth!**
> **Bless the windows, roof and floor!**
> **Bring joy to those who grace my door!**

And grant to all who enter here
Ease of sorrow, pain, and fear.
Bring rest and comfort to the tired.
Bring ease to anger—quench its fire.
Imbue this house with love and light
And laughter, joy, and sunshine, bright!
Make this home a happy place
Where all feel welcome in its space.
And see that only good befalls
Those who live within these walls.

Let the candle and incense burn out, then bring in your belongings.

◆ To Remove Negative Energy from a House

Cut a large onion into as many slices as rooms in the house. Place each slice in a dish and cover with cider vinegar, then put one of the dishes in every room in the house. After a week, dispose of the vinegar and onions in running water. (You can also use the garbage disposal to get rid of these. If you decide on this method, quarter a whole lemon and toss it into the disposal afterward. This seals the house from further negativity.)

◆ To Keep a House from Selling

This spell is particularly helpful to those who rent homes. Anoint the outer doorknobs with patchouli oil, then trace a small pentagram with the oil on the "for sale" sign. This sends prospective buyers packing.

◆ To Sell a House

> Attraction oil (see recipe
> section in chapter three)
>
> magnet

Drop a magnet into a bottle of Attraction oil, saying:

Bring a buyer
With your fire.
By magnet and metal
A house deal settle.

Let the mixture steep overnight, then use it to mark a pentagram in each corner of the "for sale" sign. Also mark a pentagram on each doorknob and rub some oil across the thresholds.

◆ To Rule a Home
To become the mistress of a home, plant rosemary by the front door. To become the master, plant St. John's wort instead.

◆ To Bring Good Luck
Continually burning a white candle in your home to honor the "spirit of the house" brings good luck and prevents negative energy accumulation.

◆ Containing Your Luck
Hang a horseshoe, points up, over the front door to keep your luck from running out.

Hunger ━━━━━━━━━━━━━━━━━━━━━━━━

◆ Winter Spell Against World Hunger

waxed paper	large spoon
1 large jar peanut butter	knife
1 small bag wild birdseed	yarn needle
large microwave-proof bowl	thin green ribbon or yarn

Cover the work area with waxed paper. Empty the peanut butter into the bowl. Put the bowl into the microwave oven for one minute, checking and stirring the peanut butter every twenty seconds. Remove it from the microwave and stir in the birdseed, adding it a little at a time. Continue adding birdseed until stirring becomes difficult.

Turn out the "dough" onto the waxed paper, and shape it into a rectangle approximately a half inch thick. Wrap the dough in waxed paper and place in the freezer for one hour.

After an hour, the dough will have "set" well enough to cut easily. (If not, return it to the freezer and check it every fifteen to twenty minutes.) Cut the dough into 2-inch squares.

Thread the needle with the yarn or ribbon. Draw the needle through the center top of a square, then cut the ribbon, leaving about 8 inches of length. Continue the process until each square has a ribbon through it. Return the squares to the freezer and leave them for twenty-four hours.

The next day, take the squares outside and tie them to tree branches for the birds to eat. When the last one is tied, open your arms to the sky and chant to the Sun and Sky:

> **I feed the birds a festive meal.**
> **I nourish them with foodstuffs real.**
> **And as they find this pleasant feast**
> **So will my human siblings eat.**
> **Remove the hunger from all life**
> **So that Your human children thrive.**
> **Give them plenty—fill them up**
> **With nourishing food on which to sup.**
> **Kill starvation, it must die**
> **This I will—by Sun and Sky!**

Hunting

Bowhunting is an ancient, sacred ritual. Because it teaches lessons in personal responsibility for the birth/death/rebirth cycle, many of us still perform this rite today. If you bowhunt, try the spells below. Their magic can do much to increase your success rate.

◆ Bowhunter's Broadhead Spell

Use this spell to ensure good broadhead flight and to bring game down swiftly.

1 juniper berry   water or oil
sharpening stone   broadheads

Crush the juniper berry and rub its juice on the
sharpening stone. Add a few drops of water or oil (or
whatever medium you normally use to sharpen your
broadheads) to the stone. As you sharpen each broadhead blade, chant:

> Berry of the forest deep
> Give to me the prey I seek.
> Let broadhead flight be smooth and true
> And sharp of cut, I ask of you.

◆ Chant for Successful Hunting

> Athena, Artemis, Diana, Pan
> Warrioress, Huntresses, and Forest God stand
> Beside me as I hunt this day
> And let good fortune come my way.
> Advise me as I stalk my prey
> In dark of woods or light of day.
> Protect me from what's seen and not
> And guide me in the perfect shot.
> So that my family's fed tonight
> Aid me, Ancients, with Your might.

◆ Spell to Bring Deer

Purchase a new bottle of vanilla extract. Remove the
cap and visualize a red light flowing from your Third
Eye and coloring the liquid in the bottle. As the light
flows into the bottle, chant:

> Where I place you, you will draw
> Deer from places near and far.
> You will bring them straight to me.
> As I will, so mote it be!

Recap the bottle and take it to your hunting spot. Sprinkle a few drops around the area where you want deer to stop.

Imagination

◆ Wildflower Seed Spell

Take a handful of wildflower seeds outside on a windy day. Hold them in your hand and empower them with the chant below.

> Wild place seeds, please free my mind.
> Let no boundaries tie or bind.
> Let dreams surface with your flight.
> Let them soar unto new heights.
> And as you find the earth, so sweet
> And root and sprout and bud and leaf
> My imagination, too, shall grow.
> As I will, it shall be so!

Then, toss them on the wind, saying:

> Imagination, now fly free!
> As I will, so mote it be!

◆ Crayon Spell

crayons	brown paper bag
cheese grater or manual pencil sharpener	clothes iron
2 sheets waxed paper	

Beginning with a color that appeals to you, use the grater or sharpener to shave some crayon pieces into the center of one of the sheets of waxed paper. Using another color, shave a bit of crayon onto the paper approximately an inch away from the first pile. Continue to make piles of crayon shavings—placing them at random—until you have an even number of piles and colors.

Cover the crayon piles with a second sheet of waxed paper and lay a brown paper bag on top. Iron over the layers with medium heat. As you iron, chant:

> **From melting wax and color flow**
> **Imagination springs and grows.**
> **It courses like a river free.**
> **As I will, so mote it be!**

Remove the paper sack and let the abstract cool. Trim the edges, and hang the picture in your work area. Use it as a meditative device whenever imagination wanes.

Inspiration

◆ Inspiration Ritual

yellow candle	incense of your choice
Creativity oil (see recipe section in chapter three)	The following Tarot cards: The Star, Ace of Rods, and The Magician

or

vegetable oil and
powdered thyme

Anoint the candle with Creativity oil or the oil and thyme mixture. Light the candle and incense. Hold The Star card to your Third Eye and say:

> **Muses, hear me! Come all Nine—**
> **Help me through this testy time**
> **And move the blocks now in my mind,**
> **So fresh perspective I can find.**

Place this card to the right of the candle.
Hold the Ace of Rods to your Third Eye and say:

> **Bring ideas where none now flow**
> **Bring new concepts; let them grow.**
> **Free me of this aggravation—**
> **Bring to me some inspiration!**

Place this card in front of the candle.

Hold The Magician to your Third Eye and say:

> **All nine Muses, come now please,**
> **And help me find that which I seek.**
> **Work together with great speed.**
> **As I will, so mote it be!**

Place this card on the left side of the candle.

Sit in front of the candle and watch the flame for a few moments. Clear your mind, relieving it of all worry and opening it for the Muses. Let the candle burn down completely.

◆ For Inspiration

Empower a piece of orange calcite by using the following chant:

> **Little stone, please now inspire**
> **The perspective I require.**
> **Bring ideas when I have need—**
> **As I will, so mote it be!**

Carry the stone with you and handle it when you lack inspiration.

◆ Inspiration for Writers

Rubbing blank paper (or the computer keyboard) with bay leaf brings inspiration to writers, authors, and poets.

◆ To Invite the Muses

Tie a bunch of thyme with a yellow ribbon and hang it above your desk or close to your work place. You could also keep a tiny yellow dish of dried thyme on your desk. This acts as a perpetual invitation for the intervention of the Muses.

―――――――――――――――――――Intuition

◆ Dark Moon Spell

Go outside during the first night of the dark Moon and chant this appeal for increased intuitive powers:

Void of blackness, darkest night,
Ruled by Crone of Power and Might,
Push my instincts into life,
So intuition grows and thrives.

Then, at bedtime, completely darken your bedroom. Draw the curtains, remove all night lights, and get into bed. Blindfold yourself and say:

Crone of Darkness, come to me
And let me feel all things unseen.

Repeat this spell each night until the first appearance of the Moon in the sky.

Jobs

◆ Spell for Getting a Raise

green candle   pen

bayberry, bergamot,   1 dollar bill
or pine oil

recent pay-check stub

Gather the spell materials together on the first night of the new Moon. Write your boss' name on the candle and below it, draw an arrow pointing down. Draw a dollar sign beneath the arrow. Below that, draw another arrow pointing down, then write your name under it (Figure 18).

Anoint the candle, while concentrating on your need for a raise. Write the amount of the raise you need below the net amount shown on the check stub and add the two together. Place this under the candle. Light the candle and visualize your boss approving a raise for you. Chant:

Figure 18.

From you to me the money flows
Casting out financial woes.
The raise I need shall be approved
Before the light of next full Moon.

Let the candle burn down completely. Wrap the wick and any wax remnants in a dollar bill and carry it with you. Ask for the raise on the Wednesday before full Moon.

--- Joy

◆ Daisy Chain Spell

To bring joy back into your life, pick a bunch of daisies. Shorten the stems to approximately 3 inches in length. With your fingernail, cut a small slit half-way down the stem of one flower and insert the next flower into the hole. Repeat the process until you have a daisy chain. While you work, chant:

> **Daisy, happy little flower,**
> **Lend your joy to me this hour.**
> **Bring your mirth into this band**
> **As I chain you with my hands.**

When the chain is long enough to slip easily over your head, securely tie the first and last stems together. Place the chain around your neck and say:

> **Daisy chain, once flowers free,**
> **Bring wildest joy now unto me.**
> **Bless me with gaiety and mirth**
> **As I live upon the Earth.**
> **And as you dry in heat and air**
> **Take with you my worries and cares.**

Wear the chain for the rest of the day, then hang it up to dry.

◆ Chrysoprase Charm

Empower a piece of chrysoprase with the following chant and carry it near your heart.

> Chrysoprase, oh happy stone,
> Let joyfulness within me roam.
> Bring a smile to heart and face;
> Let merriness my world embrace.

Judgment

◆ Crone Chant for Good Judgment

> Ancient Hag, Wise Grandmother,
> You of Wisdom, like no other,
> Help me weigh choices with precision,
> To make a good and fair decision.
> Show me what I need to see,
> Shed some light on what should be.
> And should I turn a deafened ear
> Open it so I can hear
> Help me feel what I should know.
> Show me now which way to go.
> Guide me in what I must do.
> This, Old Crone, I ask of You.

─────────────────────────── **Justice**

The chant below brings swift justice to those who treat you unfairly. Take caution in using it, though, especially if you have also behaved inappropriately. Hecate's justice knows no bounds. She sees to it that all involved get precisely what they deserve.

◆ **Chant to Hecate**

> Hecate, Dark One, hear my plea.
> Bring justice now, I ask of Thee!
> Right the wrongs that have been done,
> Avenge me now, oh Mighty One.
> Turn misfortune back to those
> Who cause my problems and my woes.
> And heap upon them karmic debt
> Lest they all too soon forget
> Their wrongful actions, words, and deeds
> Don't let them get away scot-free.
> Bring them forth from where they hide,
> Bring swift justice—wield your knife.
> Hasten, Dark One; hear my plea—
> Do what it is I ask of Thee.

Knowledge————————————

(For related spells, see "Mental Ability.")

◆ Student's Fluorite Charm

1 cup water	fluorite (alone or set in jewelry)
1 tablespoon spikenard	

Boil the water and pour it over the spikenard to make a tea. Let the tea cool to room temperature, then place the stone in the solution. (If the fluorite is set in a piece of jewelry, sprinkle it with the tea instead.) Chant:

> **Fluorite, perfect student's stone,**
> **Mix with spikenard now to hone**
> **Knowledge retention and memory skills.**
> **Be it done as I so will!**

Leave the stone for twenty-four hours, then wear it or carry it with you.

◆ For Knowledge Retention and Memory Stimulation

To retain knowledge, carry spikenard on your person. A little bit sewn into the lining or hem of a clothing article worn on the day of an exam provides remarkable results.

◆ Knowledge Retention Tea

Drink this tea during study time. Use the spikenard and water proportions listed in the Student's Fluorite

Charm on the previous page, but make the tea with the coffee maker instead. As it brews, chant:

> Spikenard herb, all knowledge ground,
> Make my memory good and sound.
> Give me firm grasp of what I learn
> So I can remember it word for word.

Sweeten the tea with honey if desired and drink.

◆ To Ward Off Forgetfulness

To ward off forgetfulness, carry a pansy on your person.

Leadership

◆ Prayer for Good Leadership Skills

> Leaders of the Ancient Ones—
> Gods and Goddesses of Moon and Sun.
> Aid me as I make my way
> On the path of leadership this day.
> Grant that I be fair and just—
> A leader that my charges trust
> Grant that I be strong but kind
> And let no glory my eyes blind.
> Help me work toward the good of all,
> Making sharp decisions and judgment calls.
> I ask You, show me how to lead—
> As I will, so mote it be!

Legal Matters───────────────────

◆ Bath for Luck in Legal Matters

3 tablespoons marigold flowers	white or purple washcloth
1 tablespoon chamomile flowers	heavy rubber band

Begin this bath on the day before your legal appointment or court date, taking one bath that day and a second on the day your appearance.

Put the marigold and chamomile in the center of the washcloth, gather the fabric ends, and secure with a rubber band. Toss it into the bathtub and turn on the warm water. As the tub fills, chant:

> **Flowers of the golden Sun**
> **Smile on me 'til this is done.**
> **Let the legal system turn my way,**
> **Keep opposing forces well at bay.**

Step into the tub and completely immerse yourself five times, saying before each immersion:

> **Legal system, be my friend.**
> **In this matter, I shall win.**

Get out of the tub and let your body dry naturally.

◆ Charm for Legal Success

Carry a pair of large hickory nuts to court in your pocket to enhance your chances of legal success. Empower them first by chanting:

> **Nuts so rich, your powers lend;**
> **Tip the scales of justice—let me win.**

◆ Court Charm

| High John the Conqueror root | 5-inch square red cloth |
| galangal | purple ribbon or yarn |

Burn a small amount of High John the Conqueror root for fourteen consecutive nights. Mix the ashes with one teaspoon of galangal and place the mixture in the center of the cloth. Gather the edges of the cloth together and secure with the ribbon. Carry the charm with you to court to gain the favor of the judge and jury.

◆ Scheduling Court Dates

For favorable results in court, ask your attorney to have your case scheduled for hearing on a Thursday.

Liberation━━━━━━━━━━━━━━━━━━━━━━━━━━

◆ Bast Chant for Liberation

> Feline Goddess, Cat-like Bast,
> Give me what I need at last.
> Scratch through mental knots that bind,
> Bring independence to my mind.
> Claw through ropes that hold me tight,
> Bring liberation to my life.
> Help me let go of what is old
> And venture forth, reborn and bold.
> Help me live my life in truth.
> Bast, I ask these things of You.

◆ Spell for Personal Freedom

Obtain a 12-inch length of thin rope or cord. The day before the dark Moon, tie it in as many knots as you can. When the night of the dark Moon arrives, take the rope outside and begin to untie the knots, saying as you loose each one:

> **Bondage has no hold on me.**
> **Darkest One, now set me free.**

When the rope is knot-free, bury it in the earth, leaving a one-inch tail above ground as a symbol of your freedom.

────────────────────────────── **Lost Items**

This chant works wonders for locating misplaced and lost items (such as car keys or eyeglasses), especially when you are in a hurry and don't have a minute to spare.

◆ **Chant for Locating Lost Items**

> Keeper of what disappears,
> Hear me now—open your ears.
> Find for me what I now seek
> By Moon, Sun, Wind, Fire, Earth, and Sea.

────────────────────────────── **Love**

◆ **Spell to Attract the Perfect Lover**

6 rose petals	rose quartz
1 teaspoon lavender	6-inch square pink cloth
1 teaspoon cinnamon	green ribbon, floss, or yarn
small piece of red ribbon (an inch or so will do)	needle and thread
1 penny	

On Friday, during the waxing Moon, place the first six ingredients in the center of the cloth. Gather the fabric edges together with your fingers and hold the pouch to your heart. Chant:

> Venus, Queen of Love, divine
> Bring the love to me that's mine.
> Perfect, she/he, and perfect, me,
> Together we are meant to be.
> Venus, Queen of Love, so warm
> Bring my love to me without harm.
> Let nothing keep us now apart,
> Bring perfect love to fill my heart.

Still holding the pouch against your heart, fill it with loving energy. Secure the pouch with green ribbon to seal the spell. Carry it on your person and sleep with it under your pillow.

When the lover comes to you, bury the pouch under a tree.

◆ Love Inviting Bath

On a Friday, place a cup of fresh, bruised yarrow leaves in a one-quart jar with a tight-fitting lid. Fill the jar with water, screw on the lid, and leave it in the refrigerator until the following Friday. On that day, before noon, strain the liquid from the leaves. Add the yarrow water to a warm bath. Stay in the tub six minutes and fully immerse yourself six times. Before each immersion, say:

> Perfect lover, come to me—
> As I will, so mote it be!

Get out of the tub and let your body dry naturally.

◆ Herbal Wine Love Spell

pink candle	¼ teaspoon allspice
Love oil	2 pinches nutmeg
1 teaspoon basil	1 cup Burgundy, Beaujolais, or other red wine
1 teaspoon dill seed	saucepan

Note: For a non-alcoholic version, instead of wine, use apple juice with a few drops of red food coloring.

On a Friday when the Moon is waxing, inscribe the candle with a pair in interlocking hearts, and anoint it with love oil. Place it near the kitchen stove and light it, saying:

> **Candle flame, burn strong and bright.**
> **From sparks of love, a flame ignite.**
> **Bring my soul mate's love to me—**
> **As I will, so mote it be!**

Place the herbs in the saucepan and pour the wine on top. Bring the mixture to a boil, then let it simmer for six minutes. As it simmers, chant over it:

> **Mix energies, herbs, spice, and wine—**
> **Call true love to me as you combine.**

Remove the mixture from the stove and let it cool. Sweeten it with honey and pour it into a glass. Before you drink the potion, blow on it six times and chant:

> **Potion of Love, flowing free,**
> **Bring hot romance at once to me.**

◆ Relationship Crystal Spell

relationship crystal

rose oil

Relationship or twin crystals (two quartz crystals that have grown together) are excellent tools to use when searching for the perfect love. Holding the crystal in your dominant hand, program it to carry out the work, then chant over it:

Separate stones, joined as one,
Find my mate by Moon and Sun.
Join us lovingly together
And let our hearts be one forever.

Dip your finger in the oil and mark two interlocking hearts on the crystal. Carry the crystal with you until the perfect mate comes to you, then store the stone in your bedroom.

◆ Spell to Rekindle Love

1 sheet parchment paper	empty wine bottle with cork
red pen	1 3-inch by 5-inch piece parchment paper
2 12-inch lengths red ribbon	

Write the following poem on the paper in red ink, but do not sign your name. Include a meeting place and time beneath the poem. (You might want to make the meeting place a public area like a nice restaurant, bar, or dance facility. Unfortunately, stalkers live in our world, too, and a secluded area may frighten the object of your desires.)

> **My heart had searched with every beat**
> **For love aflame with fiery heat,**
> **For love as soothing as the sea,**
> **For love I was not sure could be,**
> **Until the day that I saw you**
> **And foolish fear took wing and flew!**
> **Meet me, please—the time and place**
> **You'll see upon this very page**
> **And I shall guarantee your pleasure**
> **My love, my cherished, valued treasure**

Roll the paper sheet into a scroll and tie it with the ribbon. Put the scroll in the bottle and replace the cork. Write the following message retrieval instructions on the small piece of parchment paper:

> **Uncork and turn me upside down.**
> **Tap my bottom firm and sound.**
> **The scroll will slip away from me,**
> **So that its message, you can see.**

Fold the paper in half and punch a small hole in the upper corner of the folded edge. Thread the ribbon through the hole and tie it around the bottle neck. Send the bottle by courier.

◆ To Receive a Marriage Proposal

red pillar candle   orris root (powdered)

vegetable oil   anise (powdered)

orange blossoms
(can substitute
powdered yarrow)

On a Friday, inscribe the candle with your name and the name of your beloved. Draw a heart around the names and anoint the candle with vegetable oil. Combine the herbs, then roll the candle in the mixture, taking care to coat it thoroughly.

Light the candle and visualize your love proposing to you. As the candle burns, chant:

Fire of love and sex and passion

Light (name of lover)'s heart—
jolt him/her into action

So marriage he'll/she'll propose to me.

As I will so mote it be.

Let the candle burn for an hour, then snuff it out. Burn the candle for an hour on each of the next five Fridays. On the last Friday, let the candle burn down completely.

━━━━━━━━━━━━━━━━━━━━━━━━━━━━━**Luck**

◆ Good Luck Charm

Apache tear   7 star anise seeds
4-inch square yellow fabric   7 inches gold ribbon

Place the stone in the center of the fabric. Add the star anise seeds one at a time while chanting:

One for luck,
Two for money,
Three for favor,
And Four for honey.
Five for old,
And Six for new.
Seven bring success
In all that I do.

Draw up the ends of the cloth and tie the pouch with the gold ribbon. Carry the charm in your pocket or on your person.

◆ Change Your Luck Nutmeg Bath

Though this bath is said to change luck, what it really does is cleanse the aura of the negativity that draws bad luck. It also make others more accepting of your ideas, whims, and wants. Use it before employment interviews, important discussions, or before meetings with those you feel may be unresponsive.

Using a coffee filter, place 6 teaspoons of ground nutmeg in the filter cup of the coffee maker. Add one cup of water and let the tea brew. When it is cool, draw a warm bath and add the liquid.

Stay in the tub for ten minutes and totally immerse yourself six to eight times. With each immersion, think or say:

> **Change of luck, come to me,**
> **As I will, so mote it be!**

Let your body dry naturally.

◆ Waning Moon Luck Changer

When the Moon is waning, go outside and open your arms to Her. Silently communicate your problem—how badly people treat you, how you can't seem to get ahead, and all the other rotten stuff that has been going on with you. When you can think of nothing else to tell the Moon, fervently chant:

> **Moon of finest silver, wane—**
> **Take with you bad luck and bane.**
> **As you go, so does all ill—**
> **So mote it be, Moon, as I will!**

◆ Charm to Increase Your Luck

To increase your good luck, carry three Job's tears in your pocket.

Lust

◆ Charm to Bring Lust into Your Bedroom

pencil   whole cloves

1 apple   4 toothpicks

Using the pencil, draw a circle on one side of of the apple. Draw a vertical line moving downward at the center base of the circle. Cross the vertical line with a short horizontal line half-way down. This forms an ankh or feminine symbol. Draw a diagonal line from the right edge of the circle, its origin being the point between the circle's upper center and right center edge. Mark the end of the line with an arrow. This forms a masculine symbol. Figure 19 shows how the symbol should look.

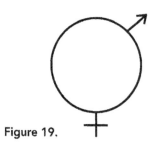

Figure 19.

Push the cloves into the apple along the pencil lines, outlining the cross first. As you work, chant:

Primordial Maiden, with this clove
Lustful urges live and grow.

Outline the arrow with cloves, saying:

> **Robust God of hoof and horn**
> **By arrow of clove, new lust is born.**

Working deosil, outline the circle with cloves while chanting:

> **Circle out and circle in—**
> **Male and female both within.**
> **This herb both enters and stays out,**
> **Lustful urges flow 'round about**
> **Touching those within this space**
> **With power that they can't escape.**
> **Clove and apple, set lust free—**
> **As I will, so mote it be!**

Push the toothpicks into the bottom center of the apple to form a stand. Place the charm on the headboard of your bed or on a bedroom windowsill.

◆ Fire of Lust Potion

1 ounce bourbon	orange juice
1 ounce vodka	1 pinch allspice
3 ounces sloe gin	

Add the first three ingredients in order to a tall glass of ice. Fill the glass with orange juice and add a pinch of allspice. As you stir, chant:

> **Fire of lust and fire of passion,**
> **Bring to me some satisfaction.**

Lust unbridled I desire,
Bring me now what I require.

Share the drink with the person you desire.

◆ To Promote Lust

To promote a lustful bedroom atmosphere, tie a sprig of white-berried mistletoe with a red ribbon and hang it above your bed. Also add a pinch each of allspice, cinnamon, and clove to the rinse water when washing bed linens.

─────────────────────────────── **Magic**

◆ Ankle Bracelet for Increased Magical Power

1 skein purple embroidery floss	cinnamon
8 skeins of embroidery floss in other colors	patchouli
purple candle	sage
vegetable oil	

Take the floss to a comfortable spot where you won't be disturbed. Grasp the ends of all nine flosses in your hand, holding them together them as one "strand." To determine the proper length, wrap the strand loosely around your ankle three times and cut. Tie the lengths together with a knot approximately two inches from the end.

Divide the length into three sections of three strands each. While concentrating on magical power growing within you, braid them together and chant:

As I braid, my magic grows.
I weave a spell to make it so.
Each cross of thread intensifies
The magic that within me lies.

Continue to braid and chant until you have a two-inch tail. Knot all nine strands together.

Anoint the candle with vegetable oil and roll it in the mixture of sage, patchouli, and cinnamon. Lay the braided piece in front of the candle. Light the candle and say:

Candle burn and add to the power
Of this charm with each passing hour.

Leave the charm until the candle burns completely. Wrap the braided strand around your ankle at least twice (three times if you are able) and tie it securely in a square knot. Wear the bracelet constantly. When you feel a new bracelet is necessary, repeat this ritual, then cut the old one off and bury it.

◆ Black Opal Charm

In many circles, the black opal is known as the "Witches' Stone" and is prized for its magic-boosting properties. To increase magical power, charge this stone with the following chant and place it on your altar before beginning magical operations.

> **Opal black, of burning fire**
> **Add the power that's required**
> **To make my magic hit its mark,**
> **By light of day, or night so dark.**

―――――――――――――**Meditation**

◆ **Meditation Ritual**

2 blue candles	sandalwood oil (vegetable oil and powdered sandalwood)
1 candle to represent yourself (you decide on the color)	

This ritual works well for people who have trouble clearing their minds enough to sink into a meditative state. You can also use it to increase communication with your Spirit Guides.

Anoint the candles with sandalwood oil. (You may substitute vegetable oil and roll the candles in sandalwood powder if you like.) During the anointing process, visualize yourself deep in a trance-like state of meditation.

Place the blue candles on either side of the candle that represents you. Light the blue candles and chant:

> Spirit Guides/Higher Self, hear my plea!
> Come now and converse with me,
> Walk with me and guide me through
> This veil of trance, I ask of you.

Light your candle and chant:

> I am surrounded by the peace of light,
> It calms and protects and brings new sight.

Sit or lie down in a comfortable position. Become aware of your breathing pattern. Inhale deeply and exhale fully. Do not force your breath. Listen to the rhythm. Feel your body relax. Close your eyes and focus on the spot between your eyes (the Third Eye).

Visualize the following colors, in order, one at a time: red, orange, yellow, green, blue, indigo, purple, and white. Hold each color to the count of five, and watch as it fades into the next color.

Still focusing on the Third Eye, "watch" your breath. See your chest rise and fall as the air flows in and out. Watch as your chest transforms into the ocean and the rhythm of your breath changes into its waves. A door appears on the water's surface. Go in and visit with your Spirit Guides/Higher Self. Ask questions. Trust the answers. Stay as long as you like.

When you are ready to return to the mundane world, walk out the door. Watch as the tides and ocean transform again into your chest and breathing pattern. Open your eyes and say:

I return to Earth again.
Thank you, Spirits, Self, and Friends.

Rise and snuff out the candles in reverse order. Put the candles in a safe place and use them again the next time you perform this ritual.

◆ To Enhance Meditation

If you use Tarot cards for meditative purposes, store a piece of sodalite with them. This charges their environment and creates an atmosphere conducive to meditation and spiritual trance.

◆ To Ease Difficulties in Meditation

If you experience difficulty in reaching a meditative state, use ametrine (substitute amethyst and citrine if you like) as a focal point. Held before and during meditation, the stone brings freedom from the physical boundaries and inhibitions that delay flight to the astral plane.

◆ Chant for Unlocking the Astral Gates

Syn, good Goddess of Locks and Doors,
Open the gates, I now implore,
Allow me to pass through the astral veil
With speed; grant fair winds to my sail.
And when I've gained what I can learn
Grant a hasty, safe return.

◆ To Fully Return from the Astral Plane

If you have difficulty returning fully from the meditative or astral state, always keep a jar of honey and a spoon nearby. When you reach that "in-between" state, grab the honey and eat a spoonful. You'll be back home in no time.

Menopause ─────────────────

◆ Hot Flash Easement Spell

2 tablespoons peppermint   honey (optional)
  (dried and crushed)

1 cup water

Place the peppermint in the filter cup of the coffee maker and add the water. As the tea brews, chant:

> **Herb of mint and spice—now tea—**
> **Of flashes hot, now make me free.**
> **Chase off night sweats so they flee.**
> **As I will, so mote it be!**

Sweeten the tea with honey if desired and drink.

◆ Menopause Celebration Ritual

2 cups sage tea (2 tablespoons sage to 1 cup water)	1 tampon or sanitary pad
1 yard black ½-inch ribbon	spoon, a stick, or any tool you can use to dig a small hole
peppermint schnapps	amethyst pendant

Note: If you prefer something non-alcoholic, substitute peppermint candy for the peppermint schnapps; diabetics may substitute peppermint tea.

Take the materials and go to a quiet beach, river, or brook. (If improvisation is necessary, go to a quiet place outdoors and pour a quart of water into the earth.) Walking deosil, cast a simple Circle and mark it by sprinkling some of the sage tea along its boundaries. Stand in the center of the Circle with your legs apart. Open your arms, throw back your head, and invoke the Crone by chanting:

> Ancient One, Grandmother,
> Wise One, Old Crone
> **And by all the names that You were once known**
> **I invite You—come now—to this festive occasion**
> **To help mark my freedom and true liberation.**

Sit down in a comfortable position. Tie the ribbon around your forehead as a headband. Dip your finger in the sage tea, and use it to mark a pentagram in the center of the band. Say:

> **Oh Crone, You bring blessings of wisdom and age,**
> **Wisdom yet to be written in book or on page.**
> **I wear this black headband in honor of You,**
> **Please guide and advise me in all that I do.**

Dip your finger in the sage tea and use it to mark a pentagram on the liquor bottle, teacup, or piece of candy. Sip the beverage or eat the candy. Say:

> **Your voice in the darkness warmed**
> **my spirit and soul.**
>
> **You embraced me and taught me**
> **the Mysteries of old.**
>
> **I drink/eat this peppermint in honor of You,**
>
> **Warm my spirit with knowledge**
> **'til my journey is through.**

Dip your finger in the sage tea and use it to mark the tampon or pad with a pentagram. Dig a small hole and bury the hygiene item. Say:

> **Your smile soothed each cramp when**
> **my moonblood was nigh.**
>
> **You promised relief when enough years passed by.**
>
> **I bury this symbol in honor of You.**
>
> **With my thanks for Your gift as I start life anew.**

Dip your finger in the sage tea and use it to mark the amethyst with a pentagram. Fasten the pendant around your neck and say:

You've given peace to my mind,
and my body, and soul.
You have led me full circle, and now I am whole.
I wear this stone in honor of You,
Grant me spiritual focus in all that I do.

Stand up and close the ritual by saying:

Ancient One, Grandmother, Wise One,
Old Crone
And by all the names that You were once known
You are welcome to go and are welcome to stay
I offer my thanks for Your presence this day.

Traveling widdershins, banish the Circle by pouring any remaining sage tea along the boundaries.

◆ Crone Ritual

black or purple candle	raven feather (substitute any black feather if necessary)
dried sage (burn as incense)	small cauldron or fireproof dish
athame or other double-edged knife	small piece of black onyx, opal, or amethyst

During the dark Moon, take the materials to a quiet place. Light the candle and the sage. Meditate upon the Crone, Her many qualities, and all the possibilities She brings with Her presence. Then breathe in

deeply through your nose and exhale fully through
your mouth. Say:

Wise and ancient, I regally rule
With a scepter of bone and scales as My tools.
I weigh cause and effect of each act of the day
And the scales tip and balance each
willful display
And karma is tallied on each dotted line
For I'm the Mistress of Lessons
and Wisdom Sublime.
Wisdom is Mine, and the balance of life
Is held in My hands as a double-edged knife
To be wielded as needed in death and rebirth
In the cycle of balance and life on the Earth.
'Tis up to Me, the life that's My own
For I am the Wise One, The Ancient—The Crone.

Take the hilt of the athame in both hands, and,
holding it above your head with the point skyward,
walk widdershins in a circle. Still holding the athame,
lower your arms and point the blade toward the
ground. Say:

I am the double-edged sword that brings
justice and fairness, death and destruction!
I am the Wise One! I am the Crone!

Brush the feather across each eyelid, then brush
it across your Third Eye. Hold the feather skyward
in both hands and walk widdershins in a circle.

Lower your arms and point the feather toward the ground. Say:

> **I am the raven of sharpest vision,**
> **Viewing even the unseen with perfect clarity!**
> **I am the Wise One! I am the Crone!**

Hold the cauldron in both hands. Touch it to your forehead, your heart, your womb, and your feet. Hold it over your head and walk widdershins in a circle. Place the cauldron between your feet. Say:

> **I am the Cauldron of Rebirth,**
> **Bubbling and boiling with life immortal!**
> **I am the Wise One! I am the Crone!**

Hold the stone in both hands. Blow on it. Rub it between your palms to warm it. Mark a pentagram on it with your saliva. Touch it to the ground. Hold the stone skyward and say:

> **I mark this portion of my journey**
> **With a symbol of the Dark Goddess,**
> **The Wise One, The Crone, Myself!**

Place the stone in front of the candle and leave it there until the candle burns completely. Carry the stone with you as a symbol of your new life.

◆ To Ease the Transition of Menopause
Wearing lavender oil as a perfume eases the transition into menopause.

Mental Ability ────────────

(For related spells, see "Knowledge.")

◆ The Mental Capacity Expansion Bath

This bath is especially helpful for students and those who find total recall of facts and figures necessary to their livelihood. For best results, take this bath weekly for a month.

Put nine unshelled hazelnuts in the filter cup of the coffee maker. Add nine cups of water and let brew. Draw a warm bath and add the tea. As you pour it into the bath, call on Mnemosyne, the ancient Muse of Memory, chanting:

> **Mnemosyne, make room for more**
> **Information; help me store**
> **All data that flows in with ease.**
> **As I will, so mote it be!**

Soak in the tub for nine minutes. While soaking, completely immerse yourself in the water nine times. Step out of the tub and let your body dry naturally.

◆ Help Store Information

Clear quartz crystals readily store information. Program one for help with mental ability, them touch it to your forehead each time you need extra brain power.

◆ To Clear Your Mind

Carry lotus root with you to help clear your mind and keep it free of mental stress.

Money

◆ Spell to Obtain Money

> green candle   basil (powdered)
> vegetable oil

Inscribe a green candle with your name and the exact amount of money you need—no more, no less. Anoint the candle with vegetable oil and roll it in powdered basil. Light it and say:

> **Money come and money grow.**
> **Money's mine; to me it flows!**

◆ Money Jar

> paper and pen   7 dimes
> quart jar with screw-on lid   bay leaf

Write your need on the paper and drop it in the jar. Take the seven dimes in your dominant hand and place them one by one into the jar. As each one drops, visualize it multiplying into huge amounts and say:

> **Toward this wish, the money grows**
> **By leaps and bounds—it overflows.**
> **Coins that jingle, coins that shine**
> **Come to me now—you are mine.**

Write your name on the back of the bay leaf and drop it into the jar. Screw the lid on tightly and put the jar in a place where you can see it every day, but a place where it is not visible to everyone who enters your home. Add a coin or two to the jar every day, and watch as money flows to you from unexpected sources. After you obtain the money you need, remove the paper and bury it outside or in a potted plant.

◆ The Money Bath
Put the 1 tablespoon of cinnamon and 4 tablespoons of parsley in the filter cup of the coffee maker. Add five cups of water and let brew. Draw a warm bath and add one cup of the tea. As you pour it into the bath, chant:

**Money come from far and near.
Money come to me! Appear!**

Completely immerse yourself in the water five times, then soak in the bath water for eight minutes. Concentrate on the improvement of your finances. Let your body dry naturally.

Take this bath on five consecutive days for best results. Use one cup of tea for each bath. Store the tea in a jar with a screw-on lid, and keep it in the refrigerator between baths.

◆ Cross-Quarter Candle Ritual
For maximum effectiveness, perform this ritual during the first minute of a cross-quarter day, one minute after midnight on February 1, May 1, August 1, or November 1 passes.

pine oil   9 white candles

gold or yellow candle   salt

6 green candles

To ensure that the spell begins at the appropriate time, anoint each candle with pine oil and arrange them on the altar the day before the ritual. Put the gold candle on the altar first. Arrange the green candles around it in a circle; then make a circle of white candles around the green ones (Figure 20).

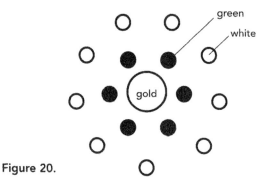

Figure 20.

At exactly one minute after midnight, pour a circle of salt around the group of candles. Light the candles, beginning with the gold one in the center. Light the green candle behind it and moving deosil, light the rest of the candles in that circle. Light the white candles in the same fashion.

Walk clockwise three times around the altar, saying with each one:

Jupiter orbit trine the Sun
And bring me money on the run.

As you watch the candles burn, meditate upon your financial needs. Visualize enough money coming to you to meet those necessities. Either let the candles burn down completely, or snuff them out in reverse order.

◆ Rumanian Money Spell

Place a small bowl or cup in a place you will see it every day. Hold three coins of any denomination in your dominant hand and say:

Trinka five, trinka five
Ancient spirits come alive.
Money grow and money thrive,
Spirits of the trinka five.

Toss the coins in the container. Repeat the spell daily, tossing three coins in the dish each day for nine consecutive days. Then continue doing the spell once a week until you have the money you need.

──────────────────────────**Negative Energy**

◆ Spell to Release Negative Energy

obsidian

rose quartz

Take the obsidian to a quiet place outside. Hold it in your dominant hand and contemplate the negativity in your life. Focus on the negativity and make it the subject of your wrath. Stomp, scream, curse, jump up and down—do whatever it takes to put yourself in an emotionally explosive state, then direct this energy into the obsidian. Fill the stone with all the nasty things in your life until there is no pain left within you.

Throw the stone as far as you can. Turn your back, take a deep breath, and walk inside.

Take the rose quartz in your receptive hand. (If you are right-handed, this is your left hand.) Sit or lie down in a comfortable position. Concentrate on the color of the rose quartz. The color is a representation of your heart. Fill the stone with love. Tell it all your joys, loves, dreams, and hopes. Carry the stone with you.

◆ Negative Energy Removal Bath

This bath is extremely useful in cleansing the body and spirit of negative energy, especially that nasty stuff that seems to come from other people. It also protects from further accumulation of negative energies.

Place six tablespoons of basil in the filter cup of the coffee maker and add one pot of water. While the

infusion brews, draw a warm bath. Pour the infusion
into the bath and chant:

> **Basil, herb of light and day,**
> **Wash negative energy completely away.**

Soak in the bath for six minutes and completely
immerse yourself four times. With each immersion,
visualize yourself being washed clean of the nasties.

◆ To Remove Negative Entities

> 9 pale blue candles (votives work well)
>
> Kyphi oil and incense (see recipe
> section in chapter three)

It is important to work this spell over nine consecutive
nights for complete effectiveness. If you miss a night,
bury the remains of the old, burned candles and start
again with new candles.

Anoint one of the candles and light the incense.
Visualize a soft blue light encasing your home and
family members. Light the candle and say:

> **Nasty critters, heed these words—**
> **Fly far away, fly like a bird.**
> **Hear me well; I now command**
> **You leave this space, this sacred land.**
> **Out, I say! I order you!**
> **Go peacefully—take flight anew.**

Let the candle burn out.

─────────────New Endeavors

(For related spells, see "Opportunity.")

◆ **Invocation to the Triple Goddess for Blessings on a New Project**

> Maiden Goddess, You Who sprout
> From tiny seed, the Earth throughout,
> Bless this project with Your joy
> And those of us in its employ.
> Mother Goddess, You Who flower
> And bring beauty to our daylight hours,
> Bless this project with Your hand
> And the fertile bounty of Your land.
> Ancient Goddess, You Who rest
> And re-seed all used things with Your breath,
> Bless us with Your intuition,
> Help bring this project to fruition.
> Bestow Your blessings, Triple One,
> And guide us 'til this project's done.

◆ **Spell for a New Beginning**

white candle	key
scissors or knife	dried iris petals or cut and sifted orris root
2- to 4-inch string or rope	dried chamomile or daisy petals
6-inch square pale green fabric	white ribbon

Write your name on the candle, then light it, saying:

> **Fresh and clean, with flame so pure,**
> **My old life is now obscure.**

Visualize in vivid detail what you expect from your new life and see new opportunities unfolding to you.

Cut the string or rope in half, letting the pieces fall on the altar. Place them in the center of the cloth square, saying:

> **Remove Your boundaries, Terminus.**
> **Liberate me, Libertus.**

Place the key in the center of the cloth square. Say:

> **Carna, come unlock Your doors,**
> **A new beginning, I implore.**

Place the iris petals or orris root in the center of the cloth square and say:

> **Iris, help me cross the bridge.**
> **Janus, give me what I wish.**

Place the daisy petals or chamomile in the center of the cloth square and say:

> **Freya, make all fresh and new,.**
> **Do now what I ask of You.**

Gather the edges of the cloth together and tie them with the ribbon to form a pouch. As you knot the ribbon, say:

A brand new life, I start today.
I seal my old life out—away.
I now embrace what comes to me
In growth and opportunity.

Let the candle burn down, then carry the pouch on your person or in your purse or briefcase.

Nightmares

◆ To Prevent Nightmares

Wash an egg in cold water and, with a pencil, write the name of the person afflicted with bad dreams. Put the egg in a dish, then place it on a nightstand close to the sleeping place of the person. If the egg cracks or breaks, flush it down the toilet. Repeat the spell until the egg stays intact for seven days. Flush the remaining egg.

◆ Citrine Nightmare Preventative

Before going to sleep, hold a citrine tightly in your dominant hand and chant:

Stone of joyful yellow light
I give my dreams to you tonight.
Grab the bad ones, the rest leave free,
So that I may dream peacefully.

Place the stone under your pillow.

◆ Dream Catchers

Dream catchers come from Native American medicine and are circular rings into which webs of fiber (usually sinew) have been woven. Placed over the bed, they trap nightmares and allow only pleasant dreams to pass into the unconscious mind. (**Note:** If you buy or make a dream catcher, make sure that the center hole is not covered by a stone or fetish. Covering that spot traps all dreams.)

◆ To End Nightmares

To eradicate nightmares, empower three mullein leaves with the following chant, then place them under your mattress.

Herb of mullein, now absorb
Unpleasant dreams before they form.
Bring to me a restful sleep.
As I will, so mote it be!

Obstacles

◆ Rosemary Vanilla Ritual

red candle   vanilla extract
vegetable oil   rosemary

Anoint the candle with vegetable oil mixed with a few drops of vanilla extract, then roll it in rosemary. Light the candle and say:

> Oh, Ancient Ones of strength and might
> Come and aid me in this plight.
> Push through all that is in my way,
> Let them fall and crumble away,
> So my path is clear and free.
> As I will, so mote it be!

As the candle burns, concentrate on the obstacles and impediments melting away as the wax itself melts. Extinguish the candle after fifteen minutes. Repeat the ritual every day for a week, letting the candle burn down completely on the last day.

◆ **To Eliminate Restrictions**

Go outside on a cloudy day and look up at the sky. Find a dense cloud and name it for the obstacle restricting your progress. Concentrate on the cloud and will it to separate. As the cloud mass dissipates, so will the obstacle.

——————————————— **Opportunity**

(For related spells, see "New Endeavors.")

◆ **Window Spell**

Beginning at the eastern-most window in your home, moisten your index finger with saliva and use it to draw a tiny pentagram in each corner of the glass pane. (If your windows have multiple panes, work with the window as a whole, placing the pentagrams in the outermost corners.) Mark an invoking pentagram in the air over the window and chant:

> **Windows of opportunity**
> **Open, open unto me.**

Working deosil, repeat the process with all the windows in your home.

Parking Places

◆ To Find a Parking Spot

When the parking lot is overcrowded and there is no place to park, try this chant. It never fails and usually provides a space close to the front door.

> **Goddess Mother, lift Your face**
> **And find for me a parking space.**

◆ To locate your parked car

If you can't remember where you parked the car, close your eyes and chant:

> **Ancients, come from near and far,**
> **Find for me my waiting car.**

Open your eyes and look out over the parking lot. The car usually comes into view right away.

Passion

◆ Spell for General Passion

Inscribe a red candle with your name, then face South and light it. Invoke the Fire Element by chanting:

> **Fire, I call upon your heat**
> **To aid me in this magical feat.**
> **Bring me what I ask of Thee.**
> **As I will, so mote it be!**

Sit in front of the candle and watch its flame dance for a few moments. Chant three times:

> **Let passion flow in me, around and about,**
> **Let its tides fill me fully, within and throughout.**
> **Grant new zest and vigor for what comes my way,**
> **And grant that I eagerly seize each new day.**

Let the candle completely burn out.

Peaceful Separation

(For related spells, see "Divorce.")

◆ The Walnut Bath

Place six unshelled walnuts in the coffee maker filter cup. Add six cups of water to the coffee maker. While the brew drips, visualize the person or persons you wish would go out of your life. Chant several times:

> **Connections rip; connections break—**
> **A peaceful life for all, please make.**

When the cycle is complete, remove the walnuts from the filter and add them to the pot. Leave the mixture to warm for three hours. After the allotted time, remove the walnuts and throw them away.

Draw a warm bath and add the separation infusion. Totally immerse yourself in the infused water seven times. With each immersion, see every touch and trace of the person being washed from your life. After the seven immersions, stay in the water for eight minutes. Allow your body to dry naturally.

◆ **For Peaceful Separation**

Take a piece of black onyx in both hands and hold it against your Third Eye. Visualize the person you wish to separate from moving away from you and finding a new direction in life. Chant:

> **As light from dark,**
> **As night from day,**
> **Leave me now,**
> **Love light your way.**
> **Walk your path**
> **And I'll walk mine.**
> **May peace and luck**
> **Upon you, shine.**

Give the stone to that person as a gift.

◆ To Keep a Former Lover from Bothering You

Cut a heart from red paper. Write your name on one half of it and your former lover's name on the other. Fold the heart in two, then tear it in half. Put away the half with your name on it for safekeeping. Either bury the other side of the heart or mail it to your former lover. He or she won't bother you again.

Pets

◆ Protective Blessing for Dogs

Diana, Goddess of the Wild,
Keeper of dogs both fierce and mild,
Hold (name of pet) safely in Your arms
And protect this creature from all harm.
And should the day come that he/she roams
Guide him/her to the path back home.
Bless (name of pet) with a joyful life
Free of hardship, stress, and strife.

◆ Protective Blessing for Cats

Bast of beauty and of grace,
Protectress of the feline race,
Shield (name of pet) from all hurt and harm
And keep him/her always safe and warm.
Watch over (name of pet) from day to day,
And guide him/her home, if he/she should stray.
And grant him/her much happiness
And a good life free of strife and stress.

◆ To Keep Fleas Away from Dogs and Cats

Create a flea dip by adding two tablespoons each of powdered pennyroyal and fleabane to each cup of boiling water. Charge it using the chant for Bedding and House Powder (found below). Cool to room temperature before dipping the animal. (**Warning:** Pennyroyal can present dangers to pregnant women. If someone in your home is pregnant, please avoid this spell.)

◆ Bedding and House Powder

Powder one cup of pennyroyal and one cup of fleabane; mix well together. Charge the powder by using this chant:

> **Herbs of soothing, cooling mint**
> **Alert all fleas to heed this hint—**
> **Begone! Begone now from this place**
> **Or Death shall take you with Its grace.**

Sprinkle about the house and on the pet's bedding. (**Warning:** Pennyroyal can present dangers to pregnant women. If someone in your home is pregnant, please avoid this spell.)

◆ Psychic Protection for Pets

Affixing a hematite ring to the collar of your dog or cat protects the animal from psychic aggravation.

◆ Protective Blessing for Fish

> Oh, fishtailed Goddess, Melusine,
> One of the Watery Depths, serene,
> Protect my fish and keep them safe
> From fungus, wounds, and all ill-fate.
> Keep them free of all disease
> And let them swim with grace and ease.
> Bless them with Your loving care,
> Guard them, Melusine—hear my prayer.

◆ To Heal Fish

To heal wounds and red streaks in fish fins, add one tablespoon of charged salt for every five gallons of aquarium water. (Don't worry; it is perfectly safe for fresh water tropical fish!)

Charge the salt by chanting:

> Salt that heals and brings new life,
> Heal my fish of physical strife.

◆ Protective Blessing for Birds

> Rhiannon, flap Your wings and rise—
> Grant (name of pet) a happy life.
> Shield him/her as he/she flies about
> And protect him/her night and day, throughout.
> Wrap him/her safely in Your wings
> And give him/her happy songs to sing.

◆ To Protect Birds from Cats

Tying rue or lavender to your bird's cage protects your feathered pet from feline aggravation.

◆ Protective Blessing for Turtles

Athena—Warrioress—Mighty One
Bless (name of pet) by Moon and Sun.
Make his/her shell like armor, strong
To shield him/her well, his/her whole life long.
Protect him/her with Your mighty spear,
Grant him/her a life of fun and cheer.
And let him/her live life at his/her pace
With no fear of rush or race.

◆ Protective Blessing for Gerbils, Rats, and Mice

Rhea, Goddess of animals wild,
Bless (name of pet), my furry child.
Let his/her life be filled with play
And happiness from day to day.
Keep him/her safe from all life's harm
And let him/her live in whiskered charm.
Bless (name of pet) with Your tender care,
Oh, Gracious Rhea, hear my prayer!

◆ Protective Blessing for Snakes

Medusa of the Writhing Mane,
Bless this snake o'er whom you reign.
Protect (name of pet) as she/he slithers through
Sunlight's warmth and moonlight's cool.
Grant his/her existence be carefree.
As I will, so mote it be!

◆ Pet Death/Euthanasia Ritual

Few things in this life seem to cause as much emotional pain as the loss of a pet. Involve euthanasia, and the remorse is nearly unbearable. Guilt pays a call. All the other emotional boogymen flock around, too, just waiting for their turn to rip the grieving pet owner to shreds.

This ritual is helpful for dealing with the guilt, remorse, and sorrow associated with the death of a pet. It also helps send animal friends peacefully into the Summerland.

sandalwood incense	rose quartz
red candle	vinegar
white candle	
1 flower of your choice	honey

Light the incense and candles, and greet the Lord and Lady by saying:

> **I come to You now to release**
> **This pain and all emotional beasts**
> **That plague my heart so heavily—**
> **Take them from me—set me free!**

Name the flower for your pet. Holding it in your hand, stroke its petals and speak to your pet with love and honesty. If euthanasia was a factor, explain your reasons for terminating his/her life cycle. If not, this is a good time to talk to your pet about the loneliness you feel without him/her.

Place the flower on the altar and lay the rose quartz on top of it. Tell your pet that the stone will always represent him/her to you, and explain that she or he is free to go to the Summerland for rebirthing. Say:

You're free to go now, Little One,
Rejoice and play—the time has come
For your spirit to be on its way.
Have fun, be happy—your love will stay!

Meditate on the spirit of your pet moving on, then place a drop of vinegar on your tongue to represent the sourness we feel when Death takes a loved one. Take some time to grieve for what might have been. (If you haven't had a good cry yet, now is the time. Scream, yell, and throw a fit if you need to, but get it all out of your system.)

When you feel you can cry no more, taste the honey. Rejoice and celebrate the relationship you had with your pet. Remember all the good times you had, the love you shared, and the special spot the pet filled in your life.

Extinguish the candles and thank the Lord and Lady for Their comforting presence.

Release the flower into a body of water, such as a river or stream. Wish it a fond farewell as it floats away. Keep the stone close to you or put it in a safe place.

———— Premenstrual Syndrome (PMS)

◆ Cramp Alleviating Tea

To stop menstrual cramps, drink a half cup of the following tea twice a day.

Place one teaspoon of feverfew in the filter cup of the coffee maker and add one cup of water. As the tea brews, chant:

> **Herb and water, powers thrive,**
> **Bring your magic now to life.**

Pour the tea and sweeten with honey if desired. Before you drink it, chant over the cup:

> **Feverfew, now herbal tea,**
> **Send painful cramps away from me.**

◆ PMS Aromatherapy Spell

Perform this spell every day for a week before you start your menstrual period and for two days after menses commences.

> jasmine oil   rose oil
> lavender oil

Blend the oils, a few drops at a time, until you have a scent that pleases you. Anoint your forehead, womb, lower back, calves, and ankles, saying with each anointing:

> **Flowers, ease this body stress,**
> **Soothe nerves and bloating—give me rest.**

◆ Charm for PMS Relief

Carry a moonstone on your person beginning one week before your period and continuing through the end of your flow. Empower it by chanting:

> **Stone of Moon and Tide and Sea,**
> **Chase pain and bloating far from me.**
> **All menstrual symptoms, now relieve.**
> **As I will, so mote it be!**

Power

◆ To Gain Control Over a Situation

> purple candle   pen and paper
>
> vegetable oil   fireproof dish
>
> cayenne pepper

Inscribe the candle with your name, then draw the infinity symbol, ∞, (a horizontal figure eight) both above and below your name. Anoint the candle with vegetable oil and roll it in cayenne pepper.

Write a brief description of the situation on the paper and place it under the candle holder. Light the candle and say:

> **Wax and herb, now bring me power**
> **That grows with every passing hour.**
> **Bring control back unto me.**
> **As I will, so mote it be!**

Let the candle completely burn down, then burn the paper in the fireproof dish. Flush the ashes down the toilet.

◆ To Increase Magical Power

Carry a clear quartz crystal that has been empowered with this chant:

> Magical power, rise and grow!
> Be housed inside this crystal stone,
> So I can use it as I need.
> As I will, so mote it be!

─────────────────Problem Solving

◆ Unraveling Spell

> white candle   small knitted clothing article
>   (an old mitten or cap works well)
>
> scissors

Inscribe the candle with your problem, then draw a question mark beneath the inscription. Light the candle and say:

> Problem, problem, melt away.
> Solutions come to me today.

Snip a thread at the edge of the knitted piece and pull the yarn to unravel it. Say:

> **Knitted thread, as you unwind,**
> **Problems can no longer bind.**

Wind the yarn into a ball, saying:

> **As I smooth you to a ball,**
> **Solutions rise—come one and all.**

Alternate unraveling and winding with the appropriate chants. The solution will come by the time all the yarn is wound.

◆ Spell to Ease Problems at Work

To smooth away problems, name a wrinkled piece of fabric for the dilemma. Iron the fabric, sprinkling it with water, if necessary, until it is wrinkle-free. As you iron, repeat this chant:

> **Chaos smooth away, take flight.**
> **Solutions come with speed of light.**

Take the cloth to your work area and handle it for a few moments. The answer to the problem will come to you.

---**Protection**

◆ **Protection Jar for the Home**

assortment of threads
in different colors

small jar with
a screw-on lid

scissors

Cut the threads into 1- to 2-inch lengths. Drop them one by one into the jar, saying with each one:

Bits of thread
Protection shed.

When the jar is full, screw the lid on, lick your index finger and use it to draw a pentagram on the jar lid. Charge the jar's protective powers with the following incantation:

Oh, Hestia of the Hearth and Home,
Guard my family with Your might.
Protect them from all ills that roam
With this little jar, sealed tight.
Protect this home, oh Hestia, too,
Confine all evil to this jar.
Bring good vibrations—old and new—
And grant good will from near and far.

Place the jar in as central a location as possible in your home.

◆ The Goddess' Prayer

Use this prayer whenever you find yourself in an uncomfortable situation or you feel a need for the Lady's protection.

Gracious Goddess
Who art Maiden, Mother, and Crone,
Celebrated be Your Name.
Help me to live in peace
Upon Your Earth
And grant me safety in Your arms.
Guide me along my chosen path
And show me Your great eternal love
As I strive to be kind to those
Who don't understand Your ways
And lead me safely to Your Cauldron of Rebirth
For it is Your Spirit that lives within me
And protects me
Forever and ever.
So mote it be.

◆ Protective Invocation to Hecate

Wise Hecate, bless me please
And all that does belong to me.
Bless my work and my endeavors
Protect and keep me safe forever
From every hex and negative thought,
From every place that harm is wrought,
From every evil that's allowed,
Protect me, Wise One. Guard me now.

Help me to walk in harmony
With every stone and bird and tree,
With every creature on this Earth.
Let me live in joy and mirth
That I may always be their friend
And gain their protection 'til this life ends.
Oh, Wise Hecate, watch over me
Until my soul, at last, is freed.

◆ Onion-Garlic Protection Charm

3 onions with leaves attached

3 garlic bulbs with leaves attached

To protect your family from interference by evil spirits, braid the garlic and onion leaves together while chanting:

Layered bulbs of power and might,
Chase away all harm and spite.

Hang the bundle in the kitchen; replace it annually.

◆ General Protection

For general protection purposes, dab a bit of lavender oil behind your ears each day.

◆ Protection from Evil Spirits

Since medieval times, tassels and fringes have been used as a protective device, because they confuse and distract evil spirits.

◆ Protection from Accidents

Carrying a rowan leaf on your person protects against all manner of accidents.

◆ Charm to Ensure Privacy

Keep a mulberry or catnip leaf inside your Book of Shadows and other personal journals to protect them from the eyes of others.

Psychic Ability———————————

◆ Psychic Tea

Drink this tea during psychic and divination works.

> 1 teaspoon cinnamon   1 teaspoon rose petals
>
> 3 teaspoons mugwort   1 teaspoon yarrow*

Combine all ingredients. Use one tablespoon of mixture for every cup of boiling water. As it steeps, chant over the tea:

> **Tea of richest psychic power**
> **Enhanced awareness on me shower.**
> **Bring the visions I should see.**
> **As I will, so mote it be!**

◆ To Seek Truth

Obsidian is known in many circles as "the stone of truth." Used as a meditational device, it has the propensity to aid in psychic development. Prepare yourself for

---

* See herbal warnings, page 311.

what you might discover, though. The energies of obsidian tend to reveal all truths, even those you may not wish to see.

◆ To Receive Psychic Messages

To open a vortex through which psychic messages can easily flow, tie a bunch of mugwort with purple and white ribbons and hang it in your magical work area. Alternatively, burn dried mugwort in the area once per week.

Psychic Attack

◆ Spell to Prevent Psychic Attack

To safeguard against psychic attack, mark a pentagram on your forehead with your index finger. Visualize it radiating a neon blue color. Chant:

> Lord and Lady, twirl about,
> Guard me day and night, throughout.
> Guide me through each passing hour
> And grant me Your protective power.
> From head to toe, from sky to ground,
> Keep me safe and well and sound.

◆ Charm to Prevent Psychic Attack

To protect against psychic attack, wear a sprig of vervain or carry some of the dried herb in your pocket.

◆ Spell to Relieve Psychic Attack

Mentally build a bubble around yourself, completely covering the outer surface with mirrors. The reflective surface causes any negative energy to bounce back to its source.

◆ To Rid Yourself of Energy Vampires

1 feather for each vampire	1 stamped envelope for each person
12 inches purple ribbon	pen
purple candle anointed with vegetable oil and rolled in powdered lavender	

Note: Try to use feathers from birds of prey. Owl, hawk, or vulture feathers work well, but if they are not easily accessible, you can also try those of the blue jay, mockingbird, or grackle.

Take the ingredients to a spot where you won't be disturbed. Gather feathers into a "bouquet" and tie the quill ends together with the purple ribbon. Light the candle. Place the envelopes and pen in the center of the area, then, using the feather bouquet as a wand and traveling deosil, cast a triple Circle around them. On the first pass, say:

I am protected.

On the second pass, say:

I am powerful.

And on the third pass say:

I am free.

Sit in the center of the Circle and close your eyes. Visualize the vampires in your life standing in front of you. See the cosmic cords that connect you to them. Remove a feather from the bunch and, wielding it as a knife, sever a cord. Say:

(Name of vampire), I free myself from you.
Our cord I cut in two.
Go away!
You cannot stay.
I start my life anew.

Place the feather in an envelope and write the person's name and address on it. Repeat the process with each vampire. Then cut the ribbon into as many portions as you have envelopes and tuck a piece inside each one. Seal the envelopes.

When the last envelope is sealed, gather them all into your dominant hand and dissolve the Circle, traveling widdershins. Say:

Gone from me the stress and strife
That you've imposed upon my life.
Your power over me is gone—
By Earth, Moon, Wind, and Shining Sun.

Let the candle burn out and mail the envelopes. (Do not put a return address on them.) The energy vampires won't bother you again.

Sexual Harassment ————————————

◆ Black Onyx Spell

black marking pen   bowl of water

black onyx   8 ice cubes

saltpeter (potassium nitrate)

Using the marker, write the name or initials of the offender on the stone. Sprinkle it with saltpeter and say:

> **Your urges are now in control.**
> **Your power over me now goes.**
> **Your energy will ebb and wane.**
> **Until you stop all abuse and pain.**

Place the stone in the bowl of water, then add the ice. As you do, say:

> **Icy water, wash away**
> **(Name of offender)'s power starting now, today.**
> **Give him/her no rest until she/he sees**
> **The jerk she/he is, and lets me be.**

Put the bowl in the refrigerator. Keep it there until the offender stops the abuse or the problem is otherwise resolved. When resolution comes, flush the water down the toilet. Take the bowl outside and dig a hole. Place the stone in the hole by "pouring" it out of the bowl. (It is important that you don't touch the stone.) Cover the stone with dirt and walk away.

◆ Protection From Sexual Harassment

Wear bergamot oil as a perfume to prevent yourself from being the object of sexual harassment.

Sleep

◆ Sleep-Inducing Tea

Add one tablespoon of chamomile flowers to a cup of boiling water. As the tea steeps, chant:

> **Soothing flowers, bring to me**
> **The sleep that I so sorely need.**

Sweeten with honey if desired.

◆ To Relieve Insomnia

Tucking a small pouch of dried hops in your pillow-case also works well to relieve insomnia.

Stinging Insects

◆ To Safeguard Against the Stings of Flying Insects

Use the following chant to keep flying insects, such as mosquitoes, wasps, bees, yellow jackets, and flies, from stinging. Used as a greeting, they fly away and refuse to come within swatting distance.

> **Blessed be thy little wings;**
> **Keep far from me your hurts and stings.**

Strength

◆ Charm for Inner Strength

Empower an acorn with the following chant and carry it on your person during difficult times.

Little seed with cap so fine,
Grant your strength and make it mine.
Make me as sturdy as your tree.
As I will, so mote it be!

◆ Chant for Physical Strength

Hercules, Great Son of Zeus,
Half God, half human, please unloose
Your great strength and lend it to
Me in this thing that I must do.
Grant me now Your nerves of steel
And Your physical strength for this ordeal,
So I can complete successfully
This task that's set in front of me.

Stress

◆ Stress Relief Bath

3 tablespoons   1 tablespoon oatmeal
chamomile flowers

1 tablespoon hops   1 tablespoon comfrey leaf

2 tablespoons calendula   1 tablespoon comfrey root

Place the ingredients in the filter cup of the coffee maker and add a full pot of water. While the mixture brews, draw a warm bath. Pour the infusion into the bath water and chant:

Herbs into the water flow,
Soothe me now from head to toe.
Dissolve all stress and ease all tension,
Wash away woes and all dissension.
Cleanse me well with all your strength,
So I may now relax at length.

Soak in the tub for at least thirty minutes.

◆ Saltwater Stress Relief Spell

Fill a clear glass with water. Add three pinches of salt to the glass, stirring the water deosil after each addition. With the first pinch, say:

One pinch to calm.

With the second:

Pinch two to relax.

And with the third:

Pinch three brings power to this magical act.

Take the water to a quiet place where you won't be disturbed. Visualize all the stress and negative energy in your being gather together into an inner bundle. Hold the glass close to your mouth and little by little,

blow the contents of the bundle out into the water.
See the bundle of stress transfering from your body
as an ugly color and changing the water to the same
putrid hue. Continue to blow into the water until
you feel every bit of anger, stress, and negativity leave
your body.

When the water is saturated with your problems,
chant over the glass:

> **Changing One of Time and Grace,**
> **Negativity now erase.**
> **Transform this energy into a potion**
> **Of peaceful tranquillity and positive motion.**

Take the glass in your hands and feel the transfor-
mative power of the Creator/Creatrix well up inside
you. Watch as the water slowly changes in color, first
at the outside edges and then throughout. When the
change is complete, drink the water. Let the new,
positive energy fill you. (Drinking in the new energy
also works as a shield against further stress.)

◆ Charm to Alleviate Stress

To ease stress, either carry an amethyst on your person or keep one within a ten foot range of you. This
stone is a natural stress absorber.

◆ Tranquillity Candle

Inscribe the symbol shown in Figure 21 on one side
of a pale blue candle as follows. Draw two intersect-
ing circles in a horizontal fashion, then center a third

Figure 21.

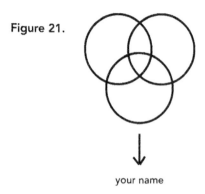

your name

circle below the two so that it intersects as well. (The intersections form a triad design.) Draw an arrow below the triad so that it points toward the bottom of the candle. Write your name beneath the arrow.

Anoint the candle with vegetable oil and roll it in lavender. Light the candle and focus upon its flame until your mind clears. Then chant:

> **Purify, oh Ancient Flame.**
> **My mind of stress, and replace the same**
> **With peace and calm tranquility/**
> **As I will, so mote it be!**

Let the candle burn for fifteen minutes, then snuff it out. Keep the candle in a safe place and repeat the spell weekly, if needed.

◆ Anti-Stress Charm

small charm bag or pouch	1 small piece each of sodalite, malachite, amethyst, and orange calcite
marker	1 tablespoon lavender

Using the marker, draw a peace sign (Figure 22) on the charm bag or pouch.

Place the lavender inside.
As you do, say:

Figure 22.

> **Lavender for great**
> **protection.**

Add the sodalite, saying:

> **Sodalite for psychic connection.**

Add the malachite, saying:

> **Malachite to bud and sprout.**

Add the amethyst saying:

> **Amethyst to calm throughout.**

Add the orange calcite, saying:

> **And calcite, orange, to amplify.**
> **Their powers mix and unify**
> **To relieve stress and aggravation,**
> **Racing heart and irritation.**

Close the bag and grip it tightly in your dominant hand. Say:

Bring me peace and calm relief.
As I will, so mote it be!

Carry the bag with you.

◆ **Tranquillity Tea**

2 tablespoons nettle	1½ teaspoons St. John's wort*
4½ teaspoons oat straw	1½ teaspoons skullcap
4½ teaspoons chamomile flowers	1½ teaspoons passion- flower

Combine the ingredients thoroughly and place three tablespoons of the mixture in the filter cup of the coffee maker. Add a full pot of water. As the tea brews and drips into the pot, chant:

Herbs, mix your energies
And flow now into harmony
To soothe and calm and bring new peace
With every sip I take of thee.

Drink the tea hot or over ice. Sweeten with honey.

---

* See herbal warnings, page 311.

Success

◆ To Receive the Blessings of the Sun

Rise well before daybreak and pour yourself a glass of orange juice. Taking the juice with you, go outside and sit comfortably, facing East. Just as the Sun begins to rise over the horizon, hold up the glass in salute and say:

> Oh Fiery Globe that rises high,
> I toast Your birth in dark of sky!
> I greet Your bright and shining rays
> And thank You for my life, this day!

Take a sip of the juice, then sit and meditate on the properties of the Sun and all that He brings to your daily life. Watch the Sun until He rises completely over the horizon, then chant:

> Oh, Shining Master of Success
> Shine on me today and bless
> My dream and goals with radiant power
> Upon them, success and triumph shower.

Drink the juice, kiss your hand to the Sun, and go about your day.

━━━━━━━━━━━━━━━━━━━━━━━━━Theft

◆ **To Deter Theft**

Gather together a garlic bulb and one sprig each of rosemary, juniper, and elder into a bouquet. Tie the bouquet with a length of purple ribbon and hang it over the front door. Alternatively, place a bit of the dry herb mixture in a handkerchief, gather the fabric edges together, and tie it securely with the ribbon.

◆ **Blue Flame Spell**

Visualize blue flames bursting from the end of your index finger. Use it to draw flaming pentagrams over all building entrances and exits, and any place money is stored. Chant:

> **Oh Flaming Pentagram of Protection**
> **Hinder thieves from this direction,**
> **By dancing flames so wild and free.**
> **As I will, so mote it be!**

◆ **Over the Door Charm**

Many years ago, I came across this anonymous poem and hung it over my front door as a theft deterrent. Since that time, nothing has ever left my home unless I gave it away willingly.

> **What comes to me I keep**
> **Who goes from me I free**
> **Yet against all I stand**
> **Who carry not my key**

◆ Protection for Purses and Wallets

To protect your purse or wallet from theft, stuff a bit
of gentian inside.

Time

◆ Time-Freezing Spell

This simple spell is very effective when you are running late or need to rest but don't have the time. If
you are some place where a clock is handy, put your
hands on it. If not, visualize yourself holding a clock.
Chant or think strongly:

> **Time, stand still, I order you!**
> **No minutes pass until I'm through**
> **Doing what I need to do.**
> **Time, stand still, I order you!**

◆ To Ensure Punctuality

If running late is a constant problem for you, try this.
Obtain a quartz crystal and hold it in your dominant
hand. Visualize green light streaming from your Third
Eye and pouring into the crystal. Hold the crystal
until you feel it pulsing with energy. Chant:

> **Crystal, give me energy**
> **And a good head start, so I'll be**
> **On time for everything and tardiness free.**
> **As I will, so mote it be!**

Carry the crystal with you at all times.

Traffic

◆ Charm to Avoid Receiving Unjust Traffic Citations

Keep a combination of tiger-eye, hematite, and quartz crystal in the glove box or, if you don't smoke, in the ashtray. The tiger-eye helps with "true sight"—a terrific aid for those who experience night blindness or difficulty with windshield glare. Hematite has a grounding force and dispels negativity. Clear quartz amplifies the effects of the other two stones. Before you place the stones in the vehicle, hold them in your dominant hand and chant:

Stones dispel unjust citations!
Deliver me safely to my destination.

This charm does not have the capacity to keep you from getting traffic citations that you deserve, such as tickets for speeding or running stop signs. It only protects you from the "ridiculous" tickets that police officers sometimes issue in order to meet their quota.

◆ Spell for Changing Traffic Lights from Red to Green

Before you have to stop for a signal light, focus on the red color and inhale deeply, pulling the color in with your breath. Then exhale fully in green, directing your breath at the bottom globe of the traffic light. The light will change to green.

◆ Spell for Driving in Icy Conditions

Visualize a white light of protection surrounding your vehicle. As you get in the vehicle and turn the ignition key, chant:

> Woden, Freya, hear my plea,
> Grant now what I ask of Thee.
> Make this car/truck not a sleigh—
> No slipping or sliding on my way.
> Keep me far from Loki's play;
> Grant safe travel to me this day.

Note: By changing the wording somewhat, this incantation can protect against unsafe travel conditions of any kind.

◆ Traffic Jam Easement Spell

I had this incantation taped to my car visor when I lived in Los Angeles. When chanted an odd number of times, it never failed to work.

> Gods of Movement and of Flow,
> Ease this mess that causes woe.
> Move these cars along their way
> And keep traffic moving through the day.
> Do this quickly—hurry, please—
> By winds of change, this traffic ease.

◆ Spell to Avoid Traffic Accidents

Mentally cast a protective Circle around your vehicle. Call the guardians or watchtowers, posting them in front, back, and on both sides of the vehicle. Ask for their protection.

Though a simple exercise, the effectiveness of this spell is amazing. In situations where being side-swiped is nearly unavoidable, other vehicles seem to just "bounce off" the protective cushion, leaving everyone involved unharmed.

Travel

◆ Spell for Safe Travel

candle of your color choice	vegetable oil
2 white candles	powdered sandalwood
purple candle	sandalwood incense

The candle of your color choice represents you or the person for whom the spell is performed. Inscribe your name on this "personality" candle. Anoint all the candles with vegetable oil and roll them in the powdered sandalwood.

Place the personality candle in the center of the altar, with a white candle on the left and the purple candle on the right. Place the second white candle in front of the first white one, and the incense in front of the purple candle (Figure 23, next page).

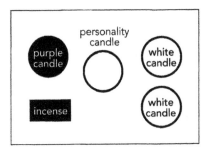

Figure 23.

Light the two white candles, the personality candle, the purple candle, and the incense—in that order. Chant the following:

> **Mother of the World, arise!**
> **Watch over me with keenest eyes.**
> **As I travel, shed Your light**
> **And keep me safe both day and night.**
> **Watch over my belongings, please,**
> **And grant my trip be filled with peace.**
> **Protect me for I am Your own,**
> **Then guide me safely back to home.**

(If this spell is for more than one traveler, substitute *we* for *I*, *us* for *me*, *our* for *my*, and so on.)

Let the candles burn down completely. Collect the burned wicks or leftover wax (if there is any) in a cloth handkerchief. Tie the upper right-hand and lower left-hand corners together, then the lower right-hand and upper left-hand corners together to secure. Carry the handkerchief with you as a safe travel charm.

◆ Luggage Arrival Charm

There is nothing worse than arriving at your destination without your luggage. Try this spell as a preventative measure.

1 yard purple ribbon or yarn	1 teaspoon lavender for each square of fabric

3-inch square white fabric
for each piece of luggage,
plus one extra

Cut the ribbon into as many pieces as you have fabric squares. Lay the fabric squares out flat and place a teaspoon of lavender in the center of each one. Gather the squares into pouches and secure the tops with the ribbon lengths. Place one pouch inside each piece of luggage. As you place each one, say:

> Lavender of sweet protection
> Guard my luggage from defection.
> Bring it safely to my destination
> Without side trip or procrastination.
> See that it arrives with me.
> As I will, so mote it be!

Carry the last pouch with you. As you place it on your person, say:

> Lavender, I take with me
> The pouch that makes this spell complete.
> This binds my luggage to me now.
> It cannot stray; it's not allowed.

◆ **Charm for Safe Journeys by Water**
To ensure a safe journey by water, carry a bit of bladderwrack and an aquamarine with you.

Unwanted Guests

◆ **To Make Unwanted Guests Leave Your Home**
Turn the household broom upside down, standing it up with the bristles pointing toward the ceiling. The guests will leave shortly.

◆ **To Keep Unwanted Guests Away from Your Home**
Before you work this spell, make sure all family members are safely inside the home. Anoint all outer doorknobs with patchouli oil and smear a little across the thresholds. Unwanted guests will stay away.

Victory

◆ **For General Victory**
Carry empowered three bay leaves on your person. Empower them by chanting:

> Laurel of the Ancient Ones,
> Let your power to me come.
> Grant success and strength to me.
> As I will so mote it be!

◆ Chant for Athletic Victory

Use the following chant before embarking upon any type of athletic competition.

> Olympic Goddesses and Gods,
> I ask You now to give a nod
> In my direction—help me win—
> Be my Aides from start to end!

◆ For Victory in Battle

Carry a piece of High John the Conqueror root to gain victory in battle. This works particularly well if your odds of winning are low. It also protects you from personal harm.

Vision

◆ Spell for Pre-cognitive Vision

purple candle	censer
vegetable oil	1 feather each from an eagle, hawk, and raven (or a small picture of each bird)
mugwort	

Anoint the candle with vegetable oil and roll it in the mugwort. Light the candle and say:

> By candle light, I now see.
> Psychic vision is set free.

Place some mugwort in the censer. Light it and say:

> **Mugwort, herb of altered state,**
> **My need for psychic vision sate.**

Gather the feathers or pictures in your dominant hand. Fan the incense smoke toward yourself, saying:

> **I call on you, Raven; I call on you, Hawk;**
> **I call on you, Eagle; fly to me—don't walk.**
> **I call on you all, three great birds of prey,**
> **To grant me your visionary powers this day.**
> **Bring me clear dreams and visions**
> **so that I may see all**
> **That shall pass in the future;**
> **let me see past the wall**
> **Of present day happenings—**
> **set my psychic eyes free,**
> **Grant perfect vision; as I will, it shall be!**

Sit in a comfortable position, close your eyes, and make a mental note to remember what the predator birds show you.

◆ To Recall Visions

To remember visions in vivid detail, carry or wear an emerald on your vision quest. Empower the stone by chanting:

> **Emerald, stone of clarity,**
> **Stone of vision, stone that sees,**
> **Grant all visions be revealed**
> **And captured to mental video reel.**

―――――――――――――――――――――**War**

◆ **Protective Prayer for Soldiers
and Those Going into Battle**

> Battle Gods and Goddesses, Ancient Ones—
> Ares, Eris, Athena, Mars, and Sun,
> Grant your protection as I go
> Into the danger of battle zones.
> Grant me Your agility and Your speed
> With sharpest skills, please guide and lead.
> Watch over me as I bravely fight
> And guard me with Your power and might.
> Oh Ancient Warriors, hear my plea!
> Unsheathe Your swords and protect me!

―――――――――――――――――――**Weather**

◆ **Spell to Bring Rain**

A broom and a small outdoor space are the only tools necessary for this spell, although a sky scattered with a few clouds is a definite plus.

Go outside, look into the sky, and invoke Oya (the African Wind Goddess) by chanting:

> Oya, Mighty One of Wind.
> I call upon You. Your breath, lend
> To blow these clouds at once together
> And bring conditions for rainy weather!

Turn your broom bristles up and "sweep" the air from West to East while willing the clouds to join together. Then invoke Thor by chanting:

> **Mighty Thor of strength and light,**
> **Your mighty fires I now invite.**
> **Bring Your lightning to the sky—**
> **The time for rainfall is now nigh.**

Repeat the sweeping motion, only this time sweep from West to South. Invoke Zeus by chanting:

> **Oh Greatest Zeus of rumbling thunder,**
> **Lend Your voice of awesome wonder.**
> **Shout it out across the skies,**
> **"Rainy weather, now arise!"**

Repeat the sweeping motion, moving the broom from West to North. Finally, invoke Melusine; chant:

> **I call upon you, Melusine,**
> **Watery Goddess, Fish-like Queen,**
> **Toss your waters in the air**
> **And fill the clouds that float up there.**

This time, start at the West and rapidly sweep the air above your head deosil. Say:

> **Raindrops fall and raindrops flow**
> **Cleanse the land so dry below.**
> **Rain until you've quenched the thirst**
> **And soothed the skin of Mother Earth!**

Rain usually comes within an hour of completing this spell.

◆ Charm to Protect the Home from Lightning

2 small rowan twigs of equal length
(2 to 3 inches long)
red thread, yarn, or ribbon

Form an equal-armed cross with the twigs. Bind the twigs in place by winding the thread around the point where they cross. Hang above your front door.

◆ Spell to Melt Ice and Snow

Go outside in the winter and dig in the frozen earth. Fill a small bowl or flower pot half full of soil. Take it in the house and work the dirt with your fingers. Invoke the Sun, chanting:

**Father Sun, come to my aid.
Bring Your warmth and shining rays.
Melt the snow and melt the ice.
Bring the Earth again to life.**

When the soil is pliable again, take it outside and face East. Scatter the soil upon the ground.

Wisdom

◆ Chant to Athena

Try this chant when you must make a decision, but aren't sure that all the facts are on the table.

> Athena, Goddess of Great Insight,
> Wisest One, take owl-like flight.
> Come to me—stay at my side
> And let Your wisdom be my guide.
> Show me what I need to see,
> So I can solve efficiently
> These problems. Lend Your expertise
> And grant Your wisdom unto me.

Wishes

◆ New Moon Wishing Novena

9 candles (use a color appro-   pen
        priate to your cause)
9 small pieces of paper

Begin this spell on the first night of new Moon and work it over nine consecutive nights. Start the novena over from the beginning if you miss a night.

Write your wish in block letters on each piece of paper and place a candle on top of each one. Light and burn one candle completely each night, while at the same time visualizing your wish coming to fruition.

◆ The Wish Sack

small piece of paper

Wishing incense (see recipe
section in chapter three)

Write your wish on a piece of paper and put some
Wishing incense on top. Lift the corners of the paper
and tightly twist them together to form a sack. Light
the wish sack, while visualizing your wish coming to
fruition. If the paper burns entirely, expect wishes to
come true immediately. Having to re-light the paper
once or twice signifies positive results but only after
obstacles clear. Having to re-light the paper any more
than twice is an indication that either your wish won't
come to pass or that what you wish isn't good for
you. (Only once have I known of this spell not bringing the desired results, and later discovered that the
practitioner wished harm to come to someone else.)

◆ Full Moon Wishing

Take nine pennies outside during the full Moon. Face
the Moon and let Her light shine upon you. Open
your arms as if to embrace the Moon and make your
request. Then say:

> You have said that when You're round
> Prayers are answered, chains unbound.
> You promise that by light of You
> All one's wishes shall come true.

Toss the pennies in Her direction, then chant:

> **Please take this token of my love,**
> **As Your silver light shines from above.**
> **Please bring me what I ask of You**
> **By darkest night and morning dew.**

Thank the Moon and leave.

◆ Vervain Wish Bath

Place 2 tablespoons of vervain in the coffee maker filter cup. Add a full pot of water. As the brew drips, concentrate on your wish and visualize it coming true. Chant:

> **Vervain, herb of wishes sweet,**
> **Bring my wish now, I entreat.**

Draw a warm bath and add the infusion to it. Completely immerse yourself nine times, saying with each immersion:

> **Wish, fly quickly unto me.**
> **As I will, so mote it be!**

Step out of the tub and allow your body to dry naturally.

◆ May Day Wish Magic

Save wax remnants from your magical candles throughout the year. On Beltane, gather them in colorful tissue paper tied with a purple ribbon. Make a fervent wish and throw the parcel into the balefire.

◆ Bay Leaf Wish Magic

Write your wish on the back of a bay leaf, then keep it in a closed box. When your wish comes true, burn the bay leaf in thanksgiving to the Ancients.

afterword

*d*uring the time it took to write this book, I found myself constantly reminded of the magical song of everyday life. Its rhythm called out to me and I danced its tune, finding true magic in areas previously mundane to me. It sang in the checkbook that balanced, the whir of the engine as a key started my car, and the way my computer booted without a hitch each morning. It chirped happily as the garbage disposal gobbled up the supper remnants and a little gray box told me who was calling before I picked up the phone. Even the impending death of a family member couldn't shut it off. It delightedly trilled right on, for death means rebirth, new life, and fresh possibilities.

As significant as these discoveries were for me, the song prompted the memory of something much more pressing. It is the most important of all the magics we find in this life; the one thing that brings true meaning to human existence and individuality. Doreen Valiente said it best when she wrote in "The Charge of the Goddess":

> **If that which you seek, you find not within,**
> **You shall never find it without....**

Yes, you are the source of life's magical melody, and its tune is up to you. The rhythm is yours, too, and depending on your choice of steps, you can either change your life or leave it just the way it is. The choice is yours—for you are the ultimate magic.

the appendices

*I*t is difficult, and often expensive, to keep an unlimited supply of spell ingredients on hand, so Appendices A and B have been added for your convenience. They contain guideline lists of herb, plant, flower, and stone substitutions, as well as their associations for magical use. This list is far from complete; in living the magical life, we constantly discover new uses for Nature's gifts and blessings. Use these lists to your advantage and feel free to substitute ingredients whenever the need arises.

For those who prefer substituting a particular god or goddess for one that is more familiar to you, Appendix C lists deities and their magical associations. For your convenience, the gender is abbreviated beside each name. Should you wish to research the origin or nationality of certain deities—or the legends that surround them— check the mythology section of your public library.

appendix a

The Magical Uses of Herbs, Plants, and Flowers

Anger Management

Almond
Catnip
Chamomile
Elecampane
Lavender
Lemon balm
Mint
Passion flower
Rose
Vervain

Anxiety Management

Skullcap
Valerian

Apathy

Ginger
Peppermint

Beauty

Avocado
Catnip
Flax
Ginseng
Maidenhair fern
Rose
Rosemary
Witch hazel

Business Success

Basil
Hawthorn

Sandalwood
Squill root

Courage

Borage
Cedar
Columbine
Masterwort
Mullein
Sweetpea
Thyme
Tonka bean
Yarrow

Depression Management

Catnip
Celandine
Daisy
Hawthorn
Honeysuckle
Hyacinth
Lemon balm
Lily of the valley
Marjoram
Morning glory
Saffron
Sheperd's purse

Divination

Camphor
Dandelion
Goldenrod

Ground ivy
Hazelnut
Henbane
Hibiscus
Meadowsweet
Mugwort
Pomegranate

Employment

Bergamot
Bayberry
Bay leaf
Pecan
Pine

Enemies

Patchouli
Slippery elm

Friendship

Lemon
Orange
Sunflower
Sweetpea
Tonka bean
Vanilla

Gambling

Buckeye
Chamomile
Pine

Gossip Management

Clove
Deerstongue
Nettle
Rue
Slippery elm
Snapdragon

Health/Healing

Allspice
Apple
Barley
Bay leaf
Blackberry
Cedar
Cinnamon
Comfrey
Elder
Eucalyptus
Fennel
Flax
Garlic
Ginseng
Golden seal
Heliotrope
Hops
Horehound
Ivy
Lemon balm
Life everlasting
Mint
Mugwort
Myrrh
Nasturtium
Nutmeg
Oak
Olive
Onion
Peppermint
Persimmon
Pine
Plantain
Rosemary
Rowan
Rue
Saffron
Sandalwood
Sheperd's purse
Thistle
Thyme
Vervain
Violet
Willow
Wintergreen
Yerba santa

Heartbreak Management

Apple
Bittersweet
Cyclamen
Honeysuckle
Jasmine
Lemon balm
Magnolia
Peach
Strawberry
Yarrow

Hunting

- Acorn
- Apple
- Cypress
- Juniper
- Mesquite
- Oak
- Pine
- Sage
- Vanilla

Legal Matters

- Buckthorn
- Celandine
- Chamomile
- Galangal
- Hickory
- High John the
  Conquerer root
- Marigold

Liberation

- Chicory
- Cypress
- Lavender
- Lotus
- Mistletoe
- Moon flower

Love

- Adam and Eve root
- Allspice
- Apple
- Apricot
- Balm of Gilead
- Basil

- Bleeding heart
- Cardamom
- Catnip
- Chamomile
- Cinnamon
- Clove
- Columbine
- Copal
- Coriander
- Crocus
- Cubeb
- Daffodil
- Daisy
- Damiana
- Dill
- Elecompane
- Elm
- Endive
- Fig
- Gardenia
- Geranium
- Ginger
- Hibiscus
- Hyacinth
- Indian paintbrush
- Jasmine
- Juniper
- Kava-kava
- Lady's mantle
- Lavender
- Lemon balm
- Lemon verbena
- Linden
- Lobelia
- Lotus
- Loveage
- Maidenhair fern

continued on page 284

Love, continued
Mandrake
Maple
Marjoram
Myrtle
Nutmeg
Orchid
Pansy
Peach
Peppermint
Periwinkle
Poppy
Primrose
Rose
Rosemary
Rue
Saffron
Skullcap
Spearmint
Spiderwort
Strawberry
Thyme
Tonka bean
Tulip
Vanilla
Vervain
Violet
Willow
Wood betony
Yarrow

Luck

Allspice
Anise
Bluebell
Calamus
China berry

Daffodil
Hazel
Heather
Holly
Job's tears
Linden
Lucky hand
Nutmeg
Oak
Orange
Persimmon
Pomegranate
Poppy
Rose
Snakeroot
Vertivert
Violet

Lust

Allspice
Caraway
Carrot
Cattail
Cinnamon
Cinquefoil
Clove
Damiana
Deerstongue
Dill
Foxglove
Galangal
Ginseng
Hibiscus
Mistletoe
Parsley
Rosemary
Sesame

Southernwood
Vanilla
Violet
Yohimbe

Menopause

Black cohosh
Lavender
Peppermint
Sage

Mental Powers

All heal
Bayleaf
Caraway
Celery seed
Forget-me-not
Hazel
Horehound
Lily of the valley
Lotus
Pansy
Periwinkle
Rue
Sandalwood
Spikenard
Summer savory
Spearmint

Nightmare Prevention

Chamomile
Mullein

Premenstrual Syndrome (PMS)

Feverfew
Jasmine
Lavender
Rose

Prophetic Dreams

Anis
Chamomile
Cinquefoil
Cloves
Heliotrope
Jasmine
Mimosa
Mint
Mugwort
Pecan
Pine
Rose
Rosemary
Snapdragon
Valerian

Prosperity

Almond
Bay leaf
Basil
Bergamot
Cedar
Chamomile
Cinnamon
Cinquefoil
Clover
Mandrake

continued on page 286

Prosperity, continued
Marjoram
May apple
Myrtle
Oak
Orange mint
Parsley
Pecan
Pine
Snapdragon
Sunflower
Sweet woodruff
Tonka bean
Tulip
Vanilla
Vervain
Wheat

Protection
African violet
Agrimony
Aloe vera
Alyssum
Angelica
Anise
Arrowroot
Asafoetida
Balm of Gilead
Basil
Bay leaf
Birch
Bladderwrack
Boneset
Bromeliad
Broom
Burdock
Cactus

Calamus
Caraway
Carnation
Cedar
Chrysanthemum
Cinnamon
Cinquefoil
Clove
Clover
Cumin
Curry
Cyclamen
Cypress
Datura
Dill
Dogwood
Dragon's blood
Elder
Elecampane
Eucalyptus
Fennel
Feverwort
Flax
Fleabane
Foxglove
Frankincense
Galangal
Garlic
Geranium
Ginseng
Heather
Holly
Honeysuckle
Horehound
Houseleek
Hyancinth
Hyssop

Ivy
Juniper
Lady's slipper
Larkspur
Lavender
Lilac
Lily
Linden
Lotus
Lucky hand
Mallow
Mandrake
Marigold
Mimosa
Mint
Mistletoe
Mugwort
Mulberry
Mullein
Mustard
Myrrh
Nettle
Oak
Olive
Onion
Parsley
Pennyroyal
Peony
Pepper
Periwinkle
Pine
Plantain
Primrose
Quince
Radish
Raspberry

Rattlesnake root
Rhubarb
Rose
Rowan
Rue
Sage
St. John's wort
Sandalwood
Snapdragon
Southernwood
Spanish moss
Sweet woodruff
Thistle
Tulip
Valerian
Vervain
Violet
Willow
Wintergreen
Witch hazel
Wolfbane
Wormwood
Wood betony
Yucca

Psychic Ability

Celery
Cinnamon
Citronella
Elecampane
Eyebright
Flax
Galangal
Honeysuckle
Lemongrass
Mace

continued on page 288

Psychic Ability, continued
Marigold
Mugwort
Peppermint
Rose
Rowan
Star anise
Thyme
Uva ursa
Wormwood
Yarrow

Sexual Harrassment Management
Bergamot
Camphor
Saltpeter
Vervain
Witch hazel

Sleep
Agrimony
Chamomile
Cinquefoil
Elder
Hops
Lavender
Linden
Peppermint
Rosemary
Sheperd's purse
Thyme
Valerian
Vervain

Strength
Acorn
Bay leaf
Carnation
Mugwort
Mulberry
Pennyroyal
Plantain
St. John's wort
Thistle

Stress Management
Calendula
Chamomile
Comfrey
Hops
Lavender
Nettle
Oats
Passion flower
St. John's wort
Skullcap

Success
Cinnamon
Clover
Ginger
High John the
   Conquerer root
Lemon balm
Orange
Rowan

Theft

Caraway
Elder
Garlic
Gentian
Juniper
Rosemary
Vetivert

Travel

Bladderwrack
Lavender

Victory

Bay leaf
High John the
  Conquerer root
Olive

Wisdom

Hazel
Rowan
Sage
Spikenard

Wishes

Bay leaf
Dandelion
Dogwood
Elder
Garlic
Gentian
Hazel
Job's tears
Juniper
Rosemary
Sage
Sunflower
Tonka bean
Vanilla
Vervain
Vetivert
Violet
Walnut

appendix b

The Magical Uses of Stones

Amplification

Calcite, orange
Quartz, crystal

Anger Management

Amethyst
Carnelian
Lepidolite
Topaz

Bad Habit Management

Moonstone
Obsidian
Onyx, black

Beauty

Amber
Cat's eye
Jasper
Opal
Quartz, rose
Unakite

Business Success

Agate, green
Aventurine
Bloodstone
Emerald
Jade
Lapis lazuli
Malachite
Tourmaline, green

Change

Ametrine
Opal
Unakite
Tourmaline,
  watermelon

Childbirth

Geode
Moonstone
Mother-of-pearl

Cleansing

Aquarmarine
Salt

Courage

Agate
Amethyst
Aquamarine
Bloodstone
Carnelian
Diamond
Hematite
Lapis Lazuli
Tiger-eye
Tourmaline,
  watermelon

Creativity

Calcite, orange
Citrine
Opal
Topaz

Depression Management

Agate, blue
Kunzite

Dieting

Moonstone
Topaz, blue

Divination

Amethyst
Azurite
Hematite
Moonstone
Obsidian, rainbow
Opal
Quartz, crystal

Dreams

Amethyst
Azurite
Citrine
Opal
Obsidian, snowflake

Eloquence

Carnelian
Celestite
Emerald

Friendship

Chrysoprase
Quartz, rose
Tourmaline, pink
Turquoise

Gambling

Amazonite
Aventurine
Tiger-eye

Gardening

Agate, green
Agate, moss
Jade
Malachite
Quartz, crystal

Grounding

Hematite
Kunzite
Moonstone
Obsidian
Salt
Black tourmaline

Healing/Health

Agate, banded
Agate, green
Amethyst
Aventurine
Azurite
Bloodstone
Carnelian

Chrysoprase
Coral
Diamond
Flint
Garnet
Hematite
Holey stones
Jade jasper
Lapis lazuli
Peridot
Petrified wood
Quartz, crystal
Quartz, smoky
Sapphire
Sodalite
Staurolite
Sugilite
Sunstone
Topaz, yellow
Turquoise

Joy

Calcite, orange
Chrysoprase
Sunstone
Unakite

Love

Alexandrite
Amber
Amethyst
Chrysocolla
Diamond
Emerald
Jade
Lapis lazuli

Lepidolite
Malachite
Moonstone
Opal
Pearl
Quartz, rose
Rhodocrosite
Sapphire
Topaz
Tourmaline, pink
Turquoise

Luck

Alexandrite
Amber
Apache tear
Aventurine
Chalcedony
Chrysoprase
Holey stones
Lepidolite
Opal
Pearl
Tiger-eye
Turquoise

Lust

Carnelian
Coral
Obsidion, mahogany
Sunstone

Magical Power

Bloodstone
Calcite, orange

Quartz, crystal
Malachite
Opal
Ruby

Meditation

Ametrine
Geodes
Hematite
Quartz, crystal
Sodalite
Sugilite

Mental Ability

Aventurine
Citrine
Emerald
Fluorite
Quartz, crystal

Nightmare Prevention

Chalcendony
Citrine
Holey stones
Lepidolite
Ruby

Peace

Agate, blue
Amethyst
Aquamarine
Aventurine
Carnelian
Chalcedony

continued on page 294

Peace, continued

Chrysocolla
Coral
Diamond
Kunzite
Lepidolite
Malachite
Obsidian
Rhodocrosite
Rodonite
Sapphire
Sodalite
Tourmaline, blue

Peaceful Separation

Onyx, black
Tourmaline, black

Physical Energy

Agate, banded
Garnet
Quartz, crystal
Rhodocrosite
Sunstone
Tiger-eye

Physical Strength

Agate, banded
Amber
Bloodstone
Cubic zirconia
Diamond
Garnet

Prosperity

Abalone
Agate, green
Aventurine
Bloodstone
Chrysoprase
Emerald
Jade
Mother-of-pearl
Malachite
Opal
Pearl
Peridot
Ruby
Sapphire
Staurolite
Tiger-eye
Tourmaline, green

Protection

Apache tear
Carnelian
Chalcedony
Chrysoprase
Citrine
Coral
Diamond
Emerald
Flint
Garnet
Holey stones
Jade
Jasper
Lapis lazuli
Lepidolite
Malachite

Marble
Moonstone
Mother-of-pearl
Obsidian
Pearl
Peridot
Petrified wood
Quartz, crystal
Ruby
Salt
Topaz, smoky
Staurolite
Sunstone
Tiger-eye
Tourmaline, black
Turquoise

Psychic Ability

Amethyst
Aquarmarine
Azurite
Citrine
Quartz, crystal
Emerald
Holey stones
Lapis lazuli

Psychic Attack Management

Alexandrite
Flourite
Hematite
Opal

Spirituality

Amethyst
Lepidolite
Sodalite
Sugilite

Stress Management

Agate, leopardskin
Amethyst
Chrysoprase
Jade
Brecciated jasper
Paua shell

Success

Amazonite
Chrysoprase
Marble

Theft Management

Cubic zirconia
Garnet

Travel

Aquarmarine
Chalcedony

Wisdom

Amethyst
Chrysocolla
Coral
Jade
Sodalite
Sugilite

appendix c

Deity Associations

The genders of the deities have been noted and abbreviated for convenience.

Business

Athena (F)
Ebisu (M)
Gaia (F)
Jupiter (M)
Midas (M)

Change

Bloedewydd (F)
Brighid (F)
Cerridwyn (F)
Epona (F)
Nemesis (F)
Persephone (F)
Rhiannon (F)

Spider Woman (F)
Vertumnus (M)

Childbirth

Aphrodite (F)
Arianrhod (F)
Brighid (F)
Demeter (F)
Gaia (F)
Hera (F)
Ilmater (F)

Communication

Amerigin (M)
Baduh (M)
Bharati(F)
Brighid (F)
Gadel (M)
Hashhye-Atlye (M)

Hermes (M)
Hu (M)
Ikto (M)
Imaluris (M)
Iris (F)
Nabu (M)
Oghma (M)
Pairikas (F)
Saravati (F)

Computers and Peripherals

Loki (M)
Murphy (M)
Thor (M)
Zeus (M)

Modems

Hermes (M)
Mercury (M)
Sarasvati (F)

Scanners

Brighid (F)
Venus (F)

Courage

Achilles (M)
Apollo (M)
Ares (M)
Artemis (F)
Athene (F)
Atlas (M)
Bellora (F)
Diana (F)
Hercules (M)

Mars (M)
Morgan (F)
Nieth (F)
Persephone (F)
Perseus (M)

Creativity

Apollo (M)
Artemis Calliste (F)
Athena (F)
Bragi (M)
Brighid (F)
Ilmater (F)
Odin (M)
Maya (F)
Minerva (F)
Muses, the (F)
Namagiri (F)
Ptah (M)
Tvashtri (M)
Veveteotl (M)
Wayland (M)

Divination

Adrste (F)
Ashtoreth (F)
Bannik (M)
Carmenta (F)
Dione (F)
Egeria (F)
Evander (M)
Filia Vocis (F)
Gaia (F)
Gwendydd (F)

continued on page 298

Divination, continued
- Inanna (F)
- Kwan Yin (F)
- Mari (F)
- Namagiri (F)
- Odin (M)
- Shamash (M)
- Thoth (M)

Fertility
- Acat (M)
- Ahurani (F)
- Aima (F)
- Althea (F)
- Amahita (F)
- Anat (F)
- Apollo (M)
- Arianrhod (F)
- Astarte (F)
- Atergatis (F)
- Baal (M)
- Bacchus (M)
- Berchta (F)
- Bona Dea (F)
- Brimo (F)
- Ceres (F)
- Cupra (F)
- Damara (F)
- Demeter (F)
- Dionsysus (M)
- Fortuna (F)
- Freya (F)
- Lono (F)
- Ma (F)
- Neith (F)
- Rhea (F)
- Wajwer (M)

Friendship
- Hathor (F)
- Maitri (F)
- Mithras (M)

Gardening
- Ceres (F)
- Rhea (F)
- Theano (F)

Gossip
- Tacita (F)

Harmony
- Alcyone (F)
- Concordia (F)
- Forseti (M)
- Harmonia (F)
- Kuan-Ti (M)
- Pax (F)

Health/Healing
- Aphrodite (F)
- Apollo (M)
- Artemis (F)
- Asclepius (M)
- Brighid (F)
- Ceadda (M)
- Diancecht (M)
- Eir (F)
- Esculapius (M)
- Gula (F)
- Hygeia (F)
- Karusepas (F)
- Kedesh (F)

Kwan Yin (F)
Liban (F)
Meditrina (F)
Rhiannon (F)
Salus (F)
Tien Kuan (M)

Heartbreak

Apollo (M)
Diana (F)
Gaia (F)
Luna (F)
Selena (F)

Home

Bannik (M)
Cardea (F)
Da-Bog (M)
Dugnai (F)
Gucumatz (M)
Hastehogan (M)
Hestia (F)
Kikimora (F)
Neith (F)
Lares, the (M)
Penates (M)
Vesta (F)

Hunting

Apollo (M)
Artemis (F)
Diana (F)
Vali (M)
Ydalir (M)

Joy

Amaterasu (F)
Ataksak (M)
Baldur (M)
Fu-Hsing (M)
Hathor (F)
Hotei (M)
Omacatl (M)
Samkhat (F)
Tien Kuan (M)

Justice

Aleitheia (F)
Anase (M)
Apollo (M)
Astraea (F)
Athene (F)
Forseti (M)
Hecate (F)
Justita (F)
Ida-Ten (M)
Kali (F)
Maíat (F)
Mens (F)
Misharu (M)
Mithras (M)
Morrigan, the (F)
Musku (M)
Syn (F)
Tyr (M)
Varuna (M)

Knowledge

- Apollo (M)
- Binah (F)
- Cerridwen (F)
- Deshtri (F)
- Gwion (M)
- Hanuman (M)
- Hecate (F)
- Hermes (M)
- Kíuei Hsing (M)
- Lugh (M)
- Ormazd (M)
- Minerva (F)
- Mnemosyne (F)
- Shing Mu (F)
- Sia (M)
- Tenjin (M)
- Toma (F)

Liberation

- Artemis (F)
- Carna (F)
- Diana (F)
- Libertas (F)
- Liberty (F)
- Terminus (M)

Love

- Amun Ra (M)
- Anat (F)
- Angus (M)
- Aphrodite (F)
- Astarte (F)
- Belili (F)
- Belit-Ilanit (F)
- Benten (F)
- Cupid (M)
- Cybele (F)
- Erzulie (F)
- Hathor (F)
- Ishtar (F)
- Isis (F)
- Kama (M)
- Venus (F)

Luck

- Agathadaimon (M)
- Benten (F)
- Bonus Eventus (M)
- Buddha (M)
- Chala (F)
- Diakoku (M)
- Felicitas (F)
- Fortuna (F)
- Gansea (M)
- Kichijo-Ten (F)
- Lakshmi (F)
- Muses, the (F)
- Tamon (M)

Lunar Workings

- Al-lat (F)
- Anumati (F)
- Artemis (F)
- Ashima (F)
- Belili (F)
- Callisto (F)
- Diana (F)
- Fati (M)
- Gou (M)
- Iah (M)

Ilmagah (M)
Jerah (F)
Levanah (F)
Luna (F)
Mah (M)
Mani (M)
Re (F)
Selene (F)

Lust

Aphrodite (F)
Arami (F)
Bes (M)
Eros (M)
Hathor (F)
Heket (F)
Indrani (F)
Isis (F)
Ishtar (F)
Lalita (F)
Lilith (F)
Min (M)
Pan (M)
Rati (F)
Venus (F)
Yarilo (M)

Magical Power

Amathaon (M)
Aradia (F)
Ayizan (F)
Cernunnos (M)
Cerridwen (F)
Circe (F)

Dakinis (F)
Demeter (F)
Diana (F)
Ea (M)
Eterna (M)
Gulleig (F)
Habondia (F)
Hecate (F)
Herodias (F)
Holle (F)
Kwan Yin (F)
Mari (F)
Odin (M)
Rangda (F)
Thoth (M)
Untunktahe (M)

Marriage

Aramati (F)
Fides (F)
Gaia (F)
Hera (F)
Ida (F)

New Endeavors

Amun Ra (M)
Apollo (M)
Brighid (F)
Cerridwyn (F)
Iris (F)
Janus (M)
Laurentina (F)
Muses, the (F)

Obstacles

Atlas (M)
Carna (F)
Janus (M)
Lilith (F)
Syn (F)
Terminus (M)

Opportunity

Brighid (F)
Carna (F)
Janus (M)
Syn (F)

Pets

Bast (F)
Diana (F)
Melusine (F)
Pan (M)
Rhea (F)
Rhiannon (F)

Power

Atlas (M)
Athena (F)
Kali (F)
Minerva (F)
Zeus (M)

Prosperity

Anna Koun (F)
Anna Perenna (F)
Benten (F)
Buddhi (F)

Daikoku (M)
Inari (M)
Jambhala (M)
Jupiter (M)
Lakshmi (F)
Ops (F)
Pluto (M)
Vasudhara (F)

Protection

Aditi (F)
Ares (M)
Atar (M)
Athena (M)
Auchimalgen (F)
Eris (F)
Hecate (F)
Kali (F)
Mars (M)
Nahmauit (F)
Padmapani (M)
Prometheus (M)
Sheila-na-gig (F)
Shui-Kuan (M)
Syen (M)
Thor (M)
Zeus (M)

Psychic Ability

Apollo (M)
Hecate (F)
Odin (M)
Psyche (F)
Rowana (F)
Thoth (M)

Solar Workings

Amaterasu (F)
Amun Ra (M)
Apollo (M)
Aya (F)
Asva (F)
Baldur (M)
Bast (F)
Bochica (M)
Da-Bog (M)
Dyaus (M)
Eos (F)
Helios (M)
Hsi-Ho (F)
Hyperion (M)
Igaehindvo (F)
Li (F)
Maui (M)
Sul (F)
Sunna (F)
Sunniva (F)
Surya (M)

Strength

Achilles (M)
Atlas (M)
Hercules (M)
Thor (M)
Zeus (M)

Success

Anu (F)
Apollo (M)
Diana (F)
Fortuna (F)

Travel

Beielbog (M)
Ekchuah (M)
Hasammelis (M)
Kunado (M)
Mercury (M)

Victory

Hercules (M)
Korraual (F)
Nike (F)
Pallus Athena (F)
Vijaya (F)
Victoria (F)

War

Ares (M)
Athena (F)
Eris (F)
Mars (M)
Thor (M)

Weather

Lightning
Agni (M)
Thor (M)
Thunor (M)
Tien Mu (F)

Rain
Agni (M)
Gwalu (M)
Mama Quilla (F)
Melusine (F)
Sadwes (F)
Tallai (F)

Snow
Father winter (M)
Holle (F)
Kris Kringle (M)

Storms
Hadad (M)
Rodasi (F)
Tempestus (F)

Thunder
Peroun (M)
Zeus (M)

Wind
Aeolus (M)
Awhiowhio (M)
Boreas (M)
Oya (F)
Sarama (F)

Wisdom
Athena (F)
Atri (M)
Baldur (M)
Bragi (M)
Buddha (M)
Dainichi (M)
Demeter (F)
Diana (F)
Ea (M)
Ekadzati (F)
Gasmu (F)
Heh (F)
Metis (F)
Minerva (F)
Namagiri (F)
Oannes (M)
Persephone (F)
Prajna (F)
Sapientia (F)
Shekinah (F)
Sophia (F)
Thoth (F)
Victoria (F)

glossary

*b*ecause magical terms aren't always "household words" to the general reading public, I have provided this glossary to define terms that may be unfamiliar.

Akasha. A force that composed of the conscious, unconscious, and subconscious minds working together. Some magical practitioners call it the Element of Spirit, Divine Power, or Higher Self.

Ankh. An Egyptian symbol of feminity. Constructed of an equal-armed cross with a circle on top, it is the astrological sign for Venus.

Asperge. To sprinkle with a liquid, usually water. Asperging involves dipping a ritual tool of some type (such as a wand, athame, bunch of herbs, or a branch) into liquid, then shaking it off onto the item to be blessed or consecrated. Circles, spaces to be consecrated, or ritual items are often asperged as part of the cleansing or blessing ceremony.

Athame. A consecrated double-edged knife, usually black-handled, used for Circle-casting, inscribing candles, and other ritual-related activities. According to most Pagan/Wiccan traditions, the athame must never be used to draw blood.

CPU. This abbreviation stands for Central Processing Unit. The CPU is actually your computer. When spells instruct you to place something on top of the CPU, just put it on top of the computer case.

Deosil. Clockwise.

Dominant Hand/Arm. This refers to the hand you use most often (for writing, picking things up with, and so on). If you are right-handed, use the right hand/arm. If you are left-handed, use the left hand/arm.

Magic. The change of any condition through ritual means.

Pentagram. An open-work five-pointed star. The pentagram is a power symbol dating back to ancient times. Some practitioners call it the "macrocosm of man," because when we stand with our feet apart and our arms extended out from our sides, we form a human star. With one point up, the pentagram symbolizes the power of the mind (Akasha) over matter (the Elements). An inverted pentagram (two points up) represents matter over mind.

Summerland. A Pagan word for the place where the Spirit resides in the afterlife. Some people think of it as the Pagan equivalent to heaven.

Taglock. An extension of the human body used to identify a person around whom a ritual or spell revolves. Common taglocks include a lock of hair, a fingernail clipping, an eyelash, or a drop of blood.

Third Eye. The point located on the forehead just above the spot between the eyebrows. Because it is believed that this area of the brain houses all components of psychic ability, many people also call this point the "psychic center." When a spell or ritual instructs you to let a particular color flow from the third eye, just visualize light of that color streaming from that location on your forehead.

Wand. A ritual Circle-casting tool made of wood, metal, or stone. Traditionally, the wand is no larger in diameter than the practitioner's thumb, and is as long as the measurement between the bend of the elbow and the tip of the middle finger.

Widdershins. Counterclockwise.

bibliography

Babcock, Michael. *The Goddess Paintings*. Rohnert Park, CA: Pomegranate Artbooks, 1994.

Beyerl, Paul. *Master Book of Herbalism*. Custer, WA: Phoenix Publishing, 1984.

Bremness, Lesley. *The Complete Book of Herbs: A Practical Guide to Growing and Using Herbs*. London: Dorling Kindersley Limited, 1988.

Brueton, Diana. *Many Moons: The Myth and Magic, Fact and Fantasy of Our Nearest Heavenly Body*. New York: Prentice Hall Press, 1991.

Budapest, Zsuzsanna E. *The Goddess in the Office: A Personal Energy Guide for the Spiritual Warrior at Work*. New York: Harper Collins Publishers, 1993.

Cunningham, Scott. *The Complete Book of Oils, Incenses, and Brews*. St. Paul, MN: Llewellyn Publications, 1989.

—————. *Cunningham's Encyclopedia of Crystal, Gem and Metal Magic*. St. Paul, MN: Llewellyn Publications, 1987.

—————. *Cunningham's Encyclopedia of Magical Herbs*. St. Paul, MN: Llewellyn Publications, 1986.

David, Judithann H., Ph.D. *Michael's Gemstone Dictionary*. Channeled by J. P. Van Hulle. Orinda, CA: The Michael Educational Foundation and Affinity Press, 1986.

Hamilton, Edith. *Mythology: Timeless Tales of Gods and Heroes*. New York: Mentor Books, 1940.

Hitchcock, Helyn. *Helping Yourself with Numerology*. West Nyack, NY: Parker Publishing Company, Inc., 1972.

Kerenyi, Karl. *Goddesses of Sun and Moon*. Translated by Murray Stein. Dallas: Spring Publications, Inc., 1979.

Kunz, George Frederick. *The Curious Lore of Precious Stones*. New York: Dover Publications, 1971.

Malbrough, Ray T. *Charms, Spells & Formulas*. St. Paul, MN: Llewellyn, 1986.

Medici, Marina. *Good Magic*. New York: Prentice Hall Press, a Division of Simon & Schuster Inc., 1989.

Melody. *Love is in the Earth: A Kaleidoscope of Crystals*. Wheat Ridge, CO: Earth-Love Publishing House, 1995.

Mickaharic, Draja. *Spiritual Cleansing: A Handbook of Psychic Protection*. York Beach, ME: Samuel Weiser, Inc., 1982.

Morrison, Sarah Lyddon. *The Modern Witch's Spellbook*. Secaucus, NJ: Citadel Press, 1971.

Nahmad, Claire. *Garden Spells.* Philadelphia: Running Press Book Publishers, 1994.

Pepper, Elizabeth and John Wilcock. *The Witches' Almanac.* Middletown, RI: Pentacle Press, Spring 1994–Spring 1995.

Renee, Janina. *Tarot Spells.* St. Paul, MN: Llewellyn Publications, 1994.

Riva, Anna. *The Modern Herbal Spellbook: The Magical Uses of Herbs.* Toluca Lake, CA: International Imports, 1974.

Slater, Herman. *The Magical Formulary.* New York: Magical Childe Inc., 1981.

Starhawk. *The Spiral Dance: A Rebirth of the Ancient Religion of the Great Goddess.* New York: Harper & Row Publishers, Inc., 1979.

Tarostar. *The Witch's Spellcraft.* Toluca Lake, CA: International Imports, 1986.

Telesco, Patricia. *Spinning Spells, Weaving Wonders.* Freedom, CA: Crossing Press, 1996.

—————. *A Victorian Grimoire.* St. Paul, MN: Llewellyn Publications, 1992.

Walker, Barbara G. *The Woman's Encyclopedia of Myths and Secrets.* New York: Harper & Rowe Publishers, Inc., 1983.

Weinstein, Marion. *Positive Magic.* Custer, WA: Phoenix Publishing, Inc., 1981.

Woolger, Jennifer Barker and Roger J. Woolger. *The Goddess Within: A Guide to the Eternal Myths that Shape Women's Lives.* New York: Ballantine Books, 1989.

Rerbal warnings

To ensure your safety, the recipes in this book have been studied by a licensed medicinal herbalist. But because every medical history is different, consult an herbalist or physician regarding interactions with prescription medications, allergies or other issues related to your individual case. The following precautions have been provided.

Those who are pregnant should consult a physician before ingesting the following herbs: Catnip, Mugwort, Roman Chamomile, Sage and Yarrow.

St. John's Wort may increase sensitivity to sunlight. Do not take this herb if you are taking MAO inhibitor drugs (certain antidepressants).

index

312